Breaking Robert's Rules

"Well written, clear, authoritative and helpful. . . . This book should revolutionize meetings everywhere—making them more productive, accessible to participants, and facilitating human communication and cooperation. . . . No one should ever go to a meeting, of any kind, anywhere, again without a copy of *Breaking Robert's Rules*."

—Carrie Menkel-Meadow,
Georgetown School of Law

"This book is revolutionary and hilarious. Revolutionary because the authors provide a new framework that will radically change the way organizations make decisions and resolve conflicts. Hilarious because it will remind the reader of every stupid or senseless meeting they've endured."

—Warren Bennis,
University of Southern California
and author of *On Becoming a Leader*

"Blessedly free of jargon and written in a brisk and positive style. . . . Can potentially make a real contribution to how people engage one another on difficult issues."

—Michael Wheeler,
Harvard Business School

"This clear guide to non-hierarchical decision-making will be a boon for churches trying to find consensus in congregational affairs rather then the traditional solution of majority rule."

—Phyllis Tickle,
author of *The Night Offices*

Breaking Robert's Rules

~

The New Way to Run Your Meeting, Build Consensus, and Get Results

Lawrence E. Susskind
AND
Jeffrey L. Cruikshank

OXFORD
UNIVERSITY PRESS

2006

OXFORD
UNIVERSITY PRESS

Oxford University Press, Inc., publishes works that
further Oxford University's objective of excellence
in research, scholarship, and education.

Oxford New York
Auckland Cape Town Dar es Salaam Hong Kong Karachi
Kuala Lumpur Madrid Melbourne Mexico City Nairobi
New Delhi Shanghai Taipei Toronto

With offices in
Argentina Austria Brazil Chile Czech Republic France Greece
Guatemala Hungary Italy Japan Poland Portugal Singapore
South Korea Switzerland Thailand Turkey Ukraine Vietnam

Published by Oxford University Press, Inc.
198 Madison Avenue, New York, NY 10016
www.oup.com

Oxford is a registered trademark of Oxford University Press

Library of Congress Cataloging-in-Publication Data
Susskind, Lawrence.
Breaking Robert's rules : the new way to run your meeting, build consensus, and get
results / Lawrence E. Susskind and Jeffrey L. Cruikshank.
p. cm.
Includes bibliographical references and index.
ISBN-13: 978-0-19-530841-9 (cloth)
ISBN-13: 978-0-19-530836-5 (pbk.)

1. Group decision-making. 2. Consensus (Social sciences). 3. Conflict management.
I. Cruikshank, Jeffrey L.
II. Title.
HM746.S87 2006   060.4'2–dc22   2006003491

Printed in the United States of America
on acid-free paper

Contents

Part 1

Overcoming the Tyranny of the Majority and
Other Problems Associated with
Robert's Rules of Order

Part 2

The Five Essential Steps in the Consensus Building Approach (CBA)

Appendices

~

Illustrations/Tables

Figures

Tables

~

Introduction

Let's begin by eavesdropping on three meetings—gatherings where important issues are at stake, and good decisions are needed.

The first takes place in a small town in the American heartland. A group has gathered at the local community center to discuss a problem related to the kids' soccer league. It's 9:00 p.m., and the meeting is heading into its second hour. The windows are steamed up. Tempers are flaring.

The meeting follows an incident a few weeks earlier, when a coach got into a shouting match with the parents of kids on the opposing team. People disagree on exactly what happened, but everyone agrees that the coach and one dad wound up face-to-face, shaking their fists and screaming obscenities at each other. The referee stepped in, called the game, and sent everyone home. A few days later, a group of parents (all from the opposing team) asked the league to replace the coach and ban him from the game. The coach countered by asking the league to ban the parents on the other side, claiming that they had baited him.

Tonight's gathering, called by the president of the league, is an unprecedented emergency meeting. Normally, the board only meets twice a year: once in the spring to finalize the fall schedule, and once in the fall to elect new officers and make arrangements for the end-of-season banquet. No one can recall a controversy at a scheduled meeting, beyond what food to serve at the banquet. Officers have been "elected" more or less by acclamation. (The truth is, it is sometimes hard to find people who want to take these jobs.) The league apparently has a set of written bylaws, but no one can find them. One board member claims that the bylaws call for the board to follow *Robert's Rules of Order*, but no one else recalls this.

It's not even clear who is on the board and who isn't. In the past, anyone who has shown up for a meeting has been welcome to participate and even vote, on those rare occasions when a vote has been taken.

Now, well into the meeting, the president of the league is getting desperate. The two camps—the supporters of the coach and the angry parents—have been hurling charges at each other since the meeting started. Nothing new is being said, but the volume level is rising. Each side suspects the president of being sympathetic to the other side, and so both are resisting his efforts to ride herd on the meeting. No one is taking notes, except the journalist in the corner whom someone has tipped off about the meeting. *Great*, the league president says to himself, *this will be in next week's paper!* No one knows if this group has the authority to fire the coach, who hasn't shown up to defend himself.

Suddenly, there's a commotion at the back of the room. The coach strides in, prompting a cascade of cheers and boos. He walks up to the big conference table and drops an envelope in front of the president. "This is a letter from my lawyer," he announces, in a voice loud enough to be heard above the din. "It says that if you take any action against me, we'll sue!"

As the crowd erupts in another round of cheering and booing, he turns and stalks out of the room.

～

Our second meeting takes place in the lunch room at a small-engine factory outside of Sacramento. The meeting has been called by the senior vice president of manufacturing from the parent company, head-quartered in Atlanta. (This is his first visit to the Sacramento facility.) He has invited a number of people to attend, including the heads of the two unions at the plant, as well as a number of salaried nonunion personnel. This latter group includes engineers, designers, the heads of Purchasing, Human Resources, and Sales and Marketing, as well as the plant manager.

The company makes engines and parts for all kinds of equipment, including lawnmowers, snow blowers, and small recreational vehicles. Up to this point, new-product development has been haphazard, at best. Most of the time, the Engineering Department decides how and when to develop a new engine model. Manufacturing, and then Purchasing, reviews and refines what Engineering comes up with. Sales and Marketing has been consulted only informally. The line workers, and their unions, are rarely consulted at all.

"I'm here to read us all the riot act," the senior vice president begins, after calling the meeting to order. Around the table, jaws set. "Let's face it," he continues. "Our product introductions have been lousy. For the most part, they've gone over budget, arrived late, and failed to perform as expected. Then, when it comes time to fix each of these problems, we don't seem to have the money or talent to get the job done.

"So what I'm asking is that this group should figure out what's wrong with what we're doing, and come up with a new way to handle project development. I'm not looking for scapegoats; I'm looking for *solutions*."

~

Our third meeting takes place in a church basement in Maine. The minister has put a notice in the church bulletin, asking members of the congregation to come together to discuss the possibility of adding a day-care program to the array of activities already sponsored by the church.

Such messages to the congregation usually generate little response, and upon arriving in the fellowship hall, the minister is amazed to see several dozen people already seated and waiting for her. She didn't think the proposal was particularly controversial, especially since she had been careful to use the words "financially self-supporting" in her description. Nevertheless, even before she can sit down, people start making their cases for and against the proposed day-care program.

Several moms practically *beg* for the church to start operating the day-care center—the sooner the better. Child-care options are too few and too expensive, they say. This is the kind of thing a church *should* be doing for its congregation and for the larger community.

But other voices weigh in as well. Some people at the meeting already run day-care programs and don't want their own church turning into a nonprofit competitor. Others worry about the increased liability that the church might be taking on. Still others, whom the minister knows to be some of the more conservative members of the congregation, want to talk about "traditional family values" and the importance of moms staying home with their children.

Hearing the increasing level of passion in people's voices and suspecting that the discussion is going nowhere fast, the minister cuts the meeting short after only a half-hour. She announces that she will bring the issue up again the following month—probably under different circumstances.

～

Are these three meetings, with their high stakes and high passions, unusual? Or are they representative of a bigger pattern?

We argue that they are indeed representative of a huge and growing problem. According to the U.S. Bureau of the Census, there are almost 40,000 cities and towns in America. Let's imagine that in each there are a half-dozen situations every year that share some of the characteristics of the soccer controversy described above—messy, emotional, confusing, painful—and perhaps involving difficult technical or regulatory issues as well. These are problems that don't seem to lend themselves to resolution through normal conversation. Yet, they cry out for solutions that are fair, efficient, wise, and stable.

The government also tells us that there are something like twenty million nonfarm businesses in the United States. Let's imagine that some percentage of these businesses—let's say one in twenty—are big and complex enough to experience organizational challenges (like the product-development problem) each year. Larger companies are likely to experience far more than one or two a year! Again, these are tough problems that simply can't be left unresolved. Many offer opportunities that shouldn't be lost. In either case, they demand new ways of looking at things, new ways of defining "success," and new ways of interacting with colleagues.

Finally, according to several organizations that market exclusively to churches, temples, and other faith-based groups, there are more than 300,000 faith-based groups in the United States. Most ministers, priests, rabbis, pastors, and other congregational leaders will readily admit that they get involved in more than a few heated debates each year, many as passionate as the child-care debate described earlier.

So no matter how you do the math, you wind up with hundreds of thousands, perhaps millions, of meetings every year in which people have to work together under difficult circumstances. Throw in all the similar situations in other countries and companies around the world, and you get *many* millions of such confrontations.

Breaking Robert's Rules is written for people in situations like these—people who need to work together, often under difficult conditions, to solve tough problems. The authors have spent many years working with people in exactly these kinds of situations, and have thought and written extensively about these experiences. The first part of the book explains why so many groups get stuck and fall back on voting and other formal ways of making decisions, like parliamentary procedure (or what is often called Robert's Rules), that create various kinds of problems. The second part summarizes the five most important steps in what is called the "consensus building approach" or CBA for short.

Consensus building is a less formal, more practical, approach to getting group agreement. Groups of any size—no matter how large or small—can use it. And anyone can learn the techniques involved. In a step-by-step and practical way, this book spells out the procedures that groups need to follow when they put aside traditional means of settling disputes—cumbersome processes that almost always leave an unhappy minority—and instead embark on a more creative and productive path that seeks nearly unanimous agreement.

The first chapter includes a capsule history of *Robert's Rules of Order*. Given how poorly suited the procedures in General Robert's book are to most group decision making, the fact that they are still around suggests that many people are not aware that there is a better alternative. CBA works because it is much less formal and much more likely to produce the best possible agreement (because it focuses on meeting everyone's interests rather than on a majority getting what it wants and a minority going home unhappy). Moreover, it is much easier to find mutually advantageous agreements than most people think, once everyone is working toward that end. The key is to get everyone into a problem-solving mode and to put aside the win–lose thinking that resides at the heart of Robert's Rules.

Part 1

~

Overcoming the Tyranny
of the Majority and Other Problems
Associated with Robert's Rules of Order

1

~

Why Break Robert's Rules?

Let's imagine that you are someone who is called upon to run a meeting and to help a group make a decision. Maybe you face a situation like one of those described in the introduction. Maybe a community program has run into a problem (these tend to generate high emotions). Maybe your company needs to attack an existing challenge in a new way. Or maybe your church is hoping to launch a new community-outreach program and is having trouble getting the new initiative organized.

Let's imagine further that you have some concerns about this upcoming meeting. Maybe you've never run a meeting and you're worried about getting the procedures right. Or maybe you suspect that there is likely to be a controversy at the meeting, and you want to make sure everyone gets a chance to be heard. Or maybe you just don't want to preside over one of those meetings that turns into an unproductive gabfest—or worse, a rock-throwing session.

How can you avoid such outcomes? You can do this through a process called **consensus building**.

Consensus building is a way for a group or organization to reach a nearly unanimous agreement, and then implement that agreement successfully. Chapter 2 provides an overview of the consensus building approach (CBA) to getting group agreement. For now, we will simply say that CBA consists of the following five steps, each of which is the subject of one of the subsequent chapters:

- **Convening.** This means agreeing to use a particular decision-making process (CBA), defining the problem, agreeing who needs to be at the table and how to get them there, and completing some of the other preliminaries for a productive dialogue.
- **Assigning roles and responsibilities.** This involves clarifying who will be in charge, specifying the ground rules, defining the role of a facilitator (i.e., either an outside professional or someone from within the group), making sure someone is keeping track of what has been decided, and laying out the rules about how observers may participate.
- **Facilitating group problem solving.** This is about generating mutually advantageous proposals and confronting disagreements in a respectful way. Effective problem solving draws upon the best available information and ensures that a range of possible solutions, including some that no one may have thought of before, are considered in an effort to do everything possible to meet the concerns of all the participants.
- **Reaching agreement.** "Deciding" isn't as simple as "voting." It's about coming as close as possible to meeting the most important interests of everyone concerned, and documenting how and why an agreement was reached.
- **Holding people to their commitments.** This involves more than each person simply doing what they promised. It's also about keeping the parties in touch with each other so that unexpected problems can be addressed together.

Maybe this strikes you as a daunting list. Maybe you're not sure that your particular problem needs all this special handling. Our response is, *it may be the only way to go!* We encourage you to suspend judgment and read on.

Consensus building means investing enough in your decision-making process to get the right people to the table, and to get the right ideas *on* the table, in ways that invite productive problem solving. It involves setting up a process that everyone agrees is open and fair. It usually calls for the involvement of some sort of facilitator, and it usually means putting in more time at the beginning of the process than in the later stages. (In previous books, we've called this "going slow to go fast.") But end-to-end, it generally takes no longer and is no more expensive than conventional group decision making. In fact, because ideas have been debated on their merits, and because decisions have been implemented in ways that are generally understood and accepted, CBA usually turns out to be not only faster but less expensive than other approaches.

And, even more important, it tends to get better outcomes, which are far less likely to come unstuck.

Let's get back to that meeting you're supposed to run.

Maybe it's not a full-fledged town meeting, with hundreds of people attempting to chart the future of the community. Rather, just a few people are involved. Whatever you're doing, though, is important enough for you and others to be devoting time and energy to the cause.

Expanding upon our scenario, let's imagine that you look up your organization's bylaws for advice on how to run the meeting. There must be some procedural requirements, right? You dig out the paperwork, open to the first section, and there you find some general material pertaining to the election of officers, the creation of committees, and so on—not very useful for your purposes.

Then you come across the following sentence:

> The parliamentary writings of General Henry M. Robert, revised, will govern the Committee's proceedings in all cases not covered by the Bylaws and Articles of Incorporation of the Committee.

What does *that* mean? Who is, or was, General Henry M. Robert? And why are his writings in charge of your meeting? The answers may surprise you.

Robert's Rules: the nineteenth-century alternative

Henry Martyn Robert was born on May 2, 1837—an American of Huguenot descent. He has been described as religious, and "squarely built but gregarious and determined." In 1867, as a thirty-year-old general in the U.S. Army Corps of Engineers, Robert was sent to San Francisco. That city, in the wake of the Gold Rush and the Civil War, and just two years before the completion of the first transcontinental railroad, was a turbulent, bustling metropolis on the move, full of dreamers and builders—in other words, full of people who sooner or later had to win the support of various groups, and perhaps to run a meeting or two.

The problem was, there was no standard way to run a meeting. Everyone had carried his or her own favorite procedures along with them to the Golden State. General Robert (who didn't much like confusion) decided to fix this problem. He decided to write a set of standard procedures for running meetings.

Robert researched the few precedents that were available. He paid special attention to the procedures followed in the U.S. House of Representatives, even though he knew that a legislative body's rules were likely to be different from the rules needed to govern a nonlegislative group. Then, in 1876, he published a set of rules for nonlegislative bodies, or "societies," to follow. "In this country," he wrote, "where customs are so slightly established and the published manuals of parliamentary practice so conflicting, no society should attempt to conduct business without having adopted some work upon the subject."

For Robert, maintaining order was the number one priority. He provided a uniform approach for conducting meetings in what has been called "a fair, orderly, and expeditious manner." He devised procedures that aim to "follow the will of the majority, protect the rights of minorities and protect the interests of those who are absent."

He even paid for the publication himself, evidently as a public service. His publisher called the slim little volume *Robert's Rules of Order*.

General Robert had definitely identified a need. Almost from the start, *Robert's Rules* was extremely popular. And until his death in 1923, nearly fifty years after the publication of his first edition, the general kept revising his little book. In subsequent years, moreover, *Robert's Rules* became something of a family business. Both his daughter and grandson, Henry M. Robert III, were involved in bringing out new editions of the book. By 1970, something like 2.6 million copies of the book had been sold.

If you go on the Web today and search "Robert's Rules," you will find an amazing number of entries. Here's one from California State University at Chico that summarizes the ten "simple rules and customs" at the heart of parliamentary procedure:

1. All members have equal rights, privileges and obligations.
2. Rules must be administered impartially.
3. Full and free discussion of all motions, reports, and other items of business is a right of all members.
4. The simplest and most direct procedure should be used.
5. Logical precedence governs the introduction and disposition of motions.
6. Only one question can be considered at a time.
7. Members may not make a motion or speak in debate until they have risen and been recognized by the chair and thus have obtained the floor.
8. No one may speak more than twice on the same question on the same day without the permission of the full assembly. No one may speak a second time on the same question if any one who has not spoken on that question wishes to do so.
9. Members must not attack or question the motives of other members. Customarily, all remarks are addressed to the presiding officer.
10. In voting, members have the right to know at all times about what motion is before the assembly and what an affirmative or negative vote means.

The list of other entries describing or interpreting parliamentary procedure is long, in part because *Robert's Rules* is now in the public domain, and a number of different publishers are trying to get you to buy their particular version. But it's also because an enormous number of organizations have adopted the *Rules* as their procedural bible.

Not to pick on any particular groups, but what do the Health Ministries Association of Roswell (Georgia), the New Hampshire Developmental Disabilities Council, the North Dakota 4-H Clubs, the Colorado Environmental Health Association, and the Boise State University Faculty have in common? They are all governed by Robert's Rules.

And they're in good company. When lawyers draw up bylaws for new foundations, nonprofits, deliberative assemblies, and other groups, they come to a box that has to be filled in, usually called "parliamentary authority," or "procedure," or something similar. Not knowing what else to put in that box, the lawyer writes "Robert's Rules."

What *are* these rules?

Henry Robert said that his rules were designed to "assist an assembly to accomplish in the best possible manner the work for which it was designed." To do so, he said, it is "necessary to restrain the individual somewhat, as the right of an individual, in any community, to do what he pleases, is incompatible with the interests of the whole."

Note that reference to "restraining the individual." We'll come back to this idea many times in the course of this book.

Most versions of the *Rules* begin with an "Order of Precedence of Motions," which defines which kind of motion is more important than another, and a "Table of Rules Relating to Motions," which claims to answer three hundred questions about parliamentary practice. This table, printed sideways, looks something like a railroad timetable, with tiny type running up, down, and sideways, and with stars in various boxes indicating what's allowable and what's not. Once you figure out this complicated table, for example, you can confirm at a glance that a motion to amend an amendment can be amended.

Don't laugh! If you're playing by Robert's Rules, you need to know that.

Collectively, these six pages were designed to serve as a crib sheet for a person running a meeting—"an epitome of parliamentary law," Robert asserted. "Everyone expecting to take an active part in meetings of a deliberative assembly should become sufficiently familiar with [them] to be able to refer to them quickly." (For an illustration of Robert's Rules at work in a deliberative assembly, see appendix D: "General Robert goes to Town Meeting.")

After that come two hundred or three hundred pages of explanation, depending on which version of the *Rules* you happen to consult.

The rules are earnest, ponderous, dense, and sometimes confusing. On the other hand, they have been used for a long time, and a great many people are perfectly comfortable with them. They reflect the mentality of an army engineer who was trying to impose order on what he saw as chaos, back in the presidency of Ulysses S. Grant. If you have ever seen a streambed that has been redirected by the Army Corps of Engineers, you will recognize the flavor of the following, which is from the wrap-up to General Robert's own preface to the 1915 edition:

> While it is important that an assembly has good rules, it is more important that it not be without some rules to govern its proceedings. It is much more important, for instance, that an assembly has a rule determining the rank of the motion to postpone indefinitely, than that it gives this motion the highest rank of all subsidiary motions except to lay on the table, as in the U.S. Senate; or gives it the lowest rank, as in the U.S. House of Representatives; or gives it equal rank with the previous question, to postpone definitely, and to commit, so that if one is pending none of the others may be moved, as under the old parliamentary law.

Did you follow that? If so, do you think it will help you run your meeting?

To be fair, the general's heart was in the right place. He didn't want the "caprice of the chairman" or the "captiousness of the members" to wreck a meeting. He wanted "order, decency, and regularity" to be the hallmarks of a "dignified public body."

We agree. We just don't think Robert's Rules gets you there.

Meetings run by Robert's Rules are driven by motions and voting. That is, once a quorum (minimum number of participants) is present and someone has asked for and "obtained the floor," that individual begins by introducing a motion (i.e., a question that will have to be voted on by the assembly). Usually, someone else is required to "second the motion," indicating that they, too, think the assembly should consider it. Then, it is placed before the whole body. That's when the debate begins. People are not only expected to speak on behalf of or against each motion, but they can offer amendments if they feel what has been proposed is inadequate. Ultimately, there must be a vote on each proposed amendment, and then, on each motion. Under certain circumstances, votes can be reconsidered. When the business of the group is concluded, the assembly adjourns.

Robert's Rules spell out in enormous detail all the possible questions that might come up and how they should be handled. For example, it enumerates different kinds of motions (i.e., privileged motions, like a request to adjourn; subsidiary motions, like a proposal to limit or extend debate; main motions (the primary business of the assembly); motions that bring a question back to the assembly for reconsideration; and incidental motions, like a point of information; and explains which motion has precedence at various points in time. In fact, most of Robert's Rules are devoted to clarifying the rules governing the consideration of each type of motion. Parliamentary procedure does not speak to what happens *before* the meeting (in terms of ensuring that representatives of all the stakeholding groups are present). It focuses solely on decision making *by majority rule* by those present.

If you are in a meeting with hundreds of strangers, perhaps a formal procedure of this sort is required to maintain order and to keep things moving along. However, if you are sitting with a dozen people in someone's living room or around an office table, it is hard to imagine that embracing this kind of formality will produce the best result.

Moreover, the business of voting on or amending motions, rather than just talking things through informally, can get in the way of effective problem solving.

What's wrong with playing by Robert's Rules?

Aside from the characteristics listed above—dense, formal, and so on—there are at least four basic problems with using Robert's Rules as the roadmap for your meeting.

The first is that General Robert felt strongly that *majority rule* should be the basic principle of decision making. Remember his notion of "restraining the individual"? Robert focused on creating a happy majority; he wasn't much concerned about the flip side of that coin, which is an unhappy minority. The unhappy minority, presumably, was just supposed to give up and go home.

In Robert's day, unhappy minorities were not nearly as powerful as they are today. Now, people who feel that an out-of-control majority has trampled upon their rights can go to court. They can go to the press and attempt to win in the court of public opinion. Or they can attempt to change the balance of power in the body that has offended them, in other words, turning themselves into the majority.

In all these cases, the result is **instability**. Things don't stick. Decisions come undone.

You may be asking yourself, "But isn't majority rule the basic premise of our democracy? Isn't it the American Way?"

Yes and no. Yes, getting 51 percent of the votes usually gives you the right to call the shots, at least for the time being. But from the start, our democracy has also been about protecting the rights of the minority. And in recent decades, thanks to a historic flood tide of lawyers, an activist judiciary, and an aggressive press corps, minorities have more levers to pull and buttons to push. Simply put, it's gotten more and more difficult to impose things on unhappy minorities.

The second problem with relying on Robert's Rules is that by doing so, your group may not get to a particularly wise decision. Think about it. There's nothing inherent in parliamentary procedure that steers a group toward practical, efficient, affordable, or broad-gauge solutions. Parliamentary procedure simply provides a way to proceed: a road map for getting from the beginning to the end of the meeting.

It's actually a little worse than that. Let's look at another realm to make this point. The game of chess rewards players who are most familiar with the rules and can apply those rules most creatively. That's fine, because (1) everybody who sits down at a chessboard knows that's what chess is all about, and (2) there's nothing earthshaking at stake in a chess game.

Not so with your meeting. If there weren't something at stake, you wouldn't be holding the meeting. The truth is, you and your group want to get to the best decision you can; you don't want to get to the fourth-best decision by strictly observing General Robert's parliamentary procedures. You want to get all the relevant information on the table, with more or less the right weight being put on each piece of the puzzle. You want a good outcome, not just a definitive result.

Good outcomes don't necessarily emerge from Robert's Rules. Why? There are lots of reasons. Questions can be framed only in certain ways. They can be changed from the way they were originally framed only when specific conditions are met. They can be voted on only one at a time, in a certain order (so possible trade-offs are very hard to consider). They can be reconsidered only under very narrow circumstances, even when new information becomes available, and even when most people in the group want an opportunity to reconsider.

The result of all this is an "all or nothing" situation: a winner-take-all outcome. No matter if there were some very good ideas in the wreckage of the losing position. That position has been vanquished, and those ideas were defeated.

The third and related problem has to do with the legitimacy of the outcome achieved through Robert's Rules. Let's assume that at this meeting you're responsible for chairing, there are three very different courses of action that might be taken. And let's assume in advance of the meeting, a majority of your fellow committee members has already decided to push one of those three solutions and has no interest in even weighing the merits of the other two. What's to prevent them from coming to the table, going through the motions—which is what the Robert's Rules procedure is about—and then voting for the solution they've already embraced?

The answer is, "nothing." As long as they're scrupulous about amending the amendment to the motion at the right time—and handling similar procedural issues correctly—they can simply show up, vote, and go home.

Again, you may be saying, "Isn't that the American Way? Isn't it all about cutting side deals away from the table, trading votes, logrolling, and so on?" Well, yes and no. Congress, like other legislative bodies, is notoriously prone to these kinds of backroom deals. On the other hand, it's unusual for a serious issue to come up for a vote on Capitol Hill with *no* debate or with no effort on the part of the proponents of a solution to make a case for that solution on the floor of the House or Senate.

Even the most cynical of logrolling politicians understands that decisions by deliberative bodies are more likely to stand up to scrutiny—of whatever kind—if the reasons behind those decisions are fully aired, in a public discussion. Debate and discussion lends legitimacy to a decision and thereby makes the decision more stable.

A final problem with Robert's Rules is that it puts too much power in the hands of the most skilled parliamentarians, that is, the process experts. General Robert wrote his rules in part to avoid what he called the "caprice of the chairman." But the rules he laid out are so dense and impenetrable that they actually encourage manipulation of the process by the few people who understand it. They allow the chairman (or anyone else who becomes an expert) to steer, channel, and limit debate.

"Everyone expecting to take an active part in meetings of a deliberative assembly should become sufficiently familiar with [the rules]," General Robert wrote. Why did he make that recommendation? Because if you don't, you can be pushed around by those who do. The game is rigged, and if you don't understand the rules *you will lose.*

A final note about voting under a majority rule system. It turns out that majority rule does not always get the majority what it wants! When there are at least three options (or candidates) in a runoff, the winner does not actually have to be the favorite of a majority of those voting. No matter which candidate wins, more of the voters might have preferred one of the other candidates. While the analysis behind this counterintuitive conclusion can get fairly complicated (indeed, Professor Kenneth Arrow won a Nobel Prize, in part, for what he called his "impossibility theorem"), this dilemma was realized as far back as the late eighteenth century when Marquis Condorcet, an expert on probability, noted the same thing. By using strategic voting, rather than sincere voting (i.e., voting for the policy or candidate that you know that your favorite will beat), it is possible to subvert the democratic intent of majoritarianism. Whoever gets to narrow the alternatives— most notably down from three to two—in essence decides what will happen.

Working in groups

Why did General Robert write his rules? Because in his experience, working in groups was difficult. We agree. And it's worth taking a few paragraphs to identify the four most important reasons why working in groups is such a challenge.

First, most people, even those in positions of responsibility, lack a basic understanding of effective approaches to group problem solving. Many people, and especially the kinds of people who are willing to put themselves in the public spotlight as leaders, tend to think that leadership is about asserting one's opinions, loudly and often.

Assuming that not everyone agrees, the result tends to be several rounds of speeches, at increasing volume and passion levels. People become exasperated. ("Why doesn't he just realize how right I am?") Before long, people start doing and saying things that *really* annoy and frustrate each other.

The second and related problem is ego. Nobody likes to lose. Especially for politicians, losing a public struggle becomes a personal defeat, which is to be avoided at all costs. (Politicians who have the smell of defeat around them are easier to defeat in the next election.)

People who have fought for and accumulated power hate to give it up. In many cases, they send mixed messages: they ask for help, and then find themselves unable to accept a solution that they didn't think of themselves. In extreme cases, a person's out-of-control ego prevents him or her from even listening to other people's ideas.

A third problem with working in groups is the winner-take-all thinking that guides many individuals and groups. It's not enough to get (almost) everything you want in a public contest; victory is far sweeter if it is coupled with a clear defeat for the other side. When the Romans finally conquered the pesky city-state of Carthage, they salted the earth so that nothing could ever grow there again. This is a classic case of winner takes all.

And finally, many groups do badly because their members have a misplaced confidence in voting, and in majority rule. We've already covered this point. Just because 51 percent of the group vote a certain way, the other 49 percent aren't likely just to roll over and take it. And the closer the vote, the more inclined the losers will be to attempt to sway a few votes and revisit the issue. At that point, you have a really difficult situation: an unstable "solution" tacked on to a controversial issue. Very few groups are prepared to deal with this kind of challenge.

Old groups, new groups

Our goal is to make this book helpful to you as you set out to create (or fix) a group process, solve a problem that requires group agreement, or run a productive meeting or series of meetings.

In that spirit, we're going to describe CBA in very simple terms and in ways that make our ideas as accessible as possible. There is a large body of literature on the subject, detailing many years of research into, and practical experience with, consensus building. Readers who are interested in more theoretical approaches, or in approaches that carry through into the later stages of consensus building—for example, helping organizations learn to get better at consensus building—should consult the reading list at the end of this book. At various points, we will compare the consensus building approach with the requirements of Robert's Rules, and you can judge for yourself the merits of each.

In the interest of accessibility, we're going to put in front of you several "real-life" groups of people. Here, we put "real life" in quotes, because these are composite stories, with the real-life players combined and disguised. But they are situations that we have actually lived through, both as participants and consensus builders.

In chapter 2, we'll talk about consensus building in the context of an ongoing group, which is most likely the circumstance in which you find yourself. What do you do when an existing group gets bogged down? For this example, we'll return to the soccer league described in our introduction, which (as it turns out) relies on Robert's Rules.

In chapter 3 and subsequent chapters, we'll talk about CBA in the context of a brand-new group. This is a less common situation, but it gives us a useful way to illustrate the basic methods and mechanics of consensus building from the ground up. We'll use a seemingly non-controversial example: a group of volunteers who have been asked by the mayor of their town to help plan a celebration. We will populate these stories with characters who "stand for" some of the kinds of people you are likely to encounter in your own group decision-making process.

In other words, just as in real life, they'll have strengths and weaknesses that can complicate things. We'll let them speak for themselves, in imaginary (but we think realistic) conversations. By listening in on these short conversations, you'll get a sense of what it's like to use our framework—even when your own cast includes some difficult characters, some of whom may even resist the consensus-building process at various points.

Appendix A provides a short checklist for anyone seeking to promote the adoption of the consensus building approach.

Key Terms Explained in Chapter 1

Robert's Rules of Order
General Henry M. Robert
Parliamentary procedure
Majority rule
Motions
Precedence of motions
Parliamentarian
Legitimacy of decision making

2

⁓

What Is Consensus?

The consensus building approach, or CBA, is not a new concept, and lots of people have at least a hazy idea of what it means. Some readers may be familiar with terms like "win/win," or "zero-sum." Some may have read *Getting to Yes*, one of the many useful books that summarize the basic principles of reaching negotiated decisions through consensual means.

But we still find lots of confusion out there in the world about consensus building. Some of that confusion begins with the word "consensus."

Defining "consensus"

Our word-processing program's dictionary defines consensus as "general or widespread agreement among all the members of a group." This is the kind of definition that should scare a sensible person away from consensus building. Anyone who has ever worked in a group knows how difficult it is to get "all the members of a group" to reach agreement on *anything*, even when you have fudge words like "general" or "widespread" thrown in. Unless the group is selected very, very carefully, achieving unanimity is like pushing a greased boulder up a hill: usually, something goes wrong along the way, with bad consequences.

So that's our first major point in this chapter: consensus building is *not* about achieving unanimity.

For our purposes, Webster's Collegiate Dictionary does a better job of defining consensus. Webster's says that consensus is (1) a *general agreement*, (2) the *judgment arrived at by most of those concerned* or (3) *group solidarity in sentiment and belief.*

So the point of this book is to define effective ways to build solidarity and agreement broadly, across your group's membership, and to get most members of the group to buy into a shared judgment by the end of the process. It's about building consensus, one brick at a time. Collectively, you work toward a shared solution. You search for something that everybody, or almost everybody, can live with. In some of our previous books, we've defined the goal of consensus building as "overwhelming agreement." Yes, you *strive for* unanimity, but when necessary, you settle for an agreement that has the support of almost all the members of your group.

This raises one more important definitional point about "consensus." It's not just about reaching overwhelming—or, against long odds, unanimous!—agreement. It's also about that agreement being reached by informed participants. However you structure your deliberations, they have to be conducted in such a way that everyone walks away from the table not just clear about what's been promised to them but also clear about what they've promised to others. So the goal is not just consensus; more accurately, it's *informed* consensus. Informed consensus means that the parties involved have agreed (overwhelmingly) that they understand exactly what's in the proposal or package, and that they can live with that proposed settlement.

The foundations and practice of consensus building

Now that we have consensus defined, let's move on to the philosophical foundations of consensus building. We have identified six such foundations:

1. **In any group or organizational effort to make decisions, it is crucial to clarify the responsibilities the people involved have to others they are presumed to speak for, or otherwise represent.**

   If the members of a group are really supposed to speak for or represent different segments of a larger community, then they should be chosen (or at least ratified) by those segments. Handpicked or "blue-ribbon" committees—appointed by a central authority and not explicitly accountable to the subgroups they are supposed to represent—are unlikely to produce anything that will be supported by everyone involved. The credibility of any problem-solving or decision-making process depends on getting legitimate representatives to the table. Sometimes members don't represent a particular segment but can still generate credibility through their positive contributions.

2. **Once a group gets together, it should not start work until its members clarify what their mission is, decide what their agenda will (and will not) include, and settle upon the ground rules that will guide their conversations.**

   Every group needs to assign responsibility for things like directing the conversation and keeping track of what has been discussed. All too often, groups that have been around for a long time forget to do this. Group effectiveness declines when participants are not self-consciously following a set of explicit ground rules and thus have no clear understanding of how to manage the group effort. Sometimes groups get stuck because their leader is not tending to the interests of the group as a whole but is focusing instead on his or her personal concerns.

3. **Before a group tries to make decisions on anything, the participants should engage in joint fact finding.**

   When people are fighting about basic information, including both facts and forecasts, it is hard to reach informed agreement. Therefore, groups have to gather information that everyone accepts as reliable (even if they interpret that information differently). This may involve putting off decisions until the group has consulted with others, including outside experts, so they can understand the likely implications of taking actions of various kinds.

4. **Groups should try to generate agreements that leave everyone better off than they would have been if no agreement had been reached.**

This is a crucial point. Most longstanding groups or committees try to get everyone to "be reasonable," and to make compromises so the group can get its work done. Most assume, at the outset, that at some point a vote will be taken, and the majority will prevail. Because they don't seek to "maximize joint gains," they almost always settle for a less desirable outcome than was possible. In our experience, most people find it hard to understand (or believe) that something other than compromise is conceivable when several contending parties are involved. But again in our experience, better outcomes can be achieved with relatively little effort. (Often, however, this requires the help of someone with mediating skills.) Voting is not usually required. Nobody needs to give up anything that they feel strongly about. The key is to engage in effective group problem solving rather than in a test of will.

5. **It is important to hold people working in groups responsible for taking a written version of a draft agreement back to the people or groups whom they represent.**

This may seem awkward in situations where long-standing committees don't involve people who actually represent the various factions or segments of a community. Even in these cases, however, it makes sense to have every committee member take a draft version of an agreement "out into the world," for discussion with others, before the full group makes a final decision. This helps enhance the legitimacy of the agreement, increases its responsiveness to the concerns and needs of the community at large, and prepares the group for implementation problems that are likely to arise.

6. Groups should always think ahead about the things that can go wrong as they try to implement whatever decisions or agreements they reach.

Consensus building groups should try to anticipate the obstacles to implementation they are likely to face, including possible surprises or changes that could pop up, and design agreements that are flexible and strong enough to withstand such challenges. Sometimes groups cut corners at this stage, either because they believe they have hit upon a good solution already or simply because they are tired. But planning for the unexpected is absolutely critical, because (1) the unexpected will happen, and (2) the group is unlikely to go back and modify the agreement after everything falls apart.

The five-step model of consensus building

Now let's translate these philosophical foundations into the specific sequence of steps involved in consensus building: the same five steps that we introduced in chapter 1. Not surprisingly, you will see a lot of overlap between the foundations described earlier and the five steps described here.

In this book, we're going to define and illustrate the five basic phases of consensus building. Each is the subject of one of the following five chapters. You will learn about each phase in some detail—that is, deeply enough to be comfortable with it—and also to be able to use these ideas creatively with your group.

Meanwhile, though, we want to be able to use some of the terms involved. So at this point, we want to provide more details about the five phases introduced in chapter 1. They are:

- Convening
- Assigning Roles and Responsibilities
- Facilitating Group Problem Solving
- Reaching Agreement
- Holding People to Their Commitments

Convening

The first step in any process of consensus building is getting the right people to the table with the right expectations. Sometimes the makeup of the group is set without reference to the particular problem. A long-standing group with a permanent membership usually has to address a wide range of issues, but it doesn't change its membership every time it has to confront a new issue. In these circumstances, it helps a lot if the standing committee has a way to gauge the detailed concerns and priorities of other relevant stakeholders, if only to know whom to consult. Usually, this requires some kind of preassessment of the interests of the parties likely to be affected by a decision that's going to be made, or who have a stake in the problem that the group is trying to solve.

Any decision-making group needs to do enough homework to understand the substance and the context of the issue or problem it is trying to address. Why is this important? Because, simply put, you need to know whose interests are at stake, whom to consult, or even whom to invite to meet with (or join) the group. You need to map the situation to identify the categories of relevant stakeholders, and wherever possible, identify people who can speak for each of those categories. You need to figure out which concern is a priority to whom. This is sometimes referred to as a "conflict assessment," or simply an "assessment." (There's not always a conflict.)

More on the assessment below. But here's a potential rub: in most cases, the person in charge of the group (i.e., the convener-leader) *should not do the assessment.* The reason is simple: the convener-leader is an interested party. How can the convener-leader be expected to be a passionate advocate for his or her own position, and at the same time, not give that position special weight in sizing up the situation and probing the concerns of all the relevant stakeholders? And even if he or she *does* pull off that amazing feat of neutrality, there are likely to be people who won't believe that he or she has pulled it off. They will look for what they consider to be evidence of a stacked deck, and people can usually find such evidence if that's what they are looking for.

So in most cases, the leader causes the assessment to be done by someone else—ideally, someone viewed as neutral by everyone involved. That neutral party talks to the stakeholders, both obvious and not so obvious, in a confidential, not-for-attribution manner. He or she draws out their concerns and interests, and carries on the work (begun by the convener) of identifying the right spokesperson for each category of stakeholders. The group then has to decide how it wants to ensure representation of all these interests in its deliberations.

Over the past several decades, facilitation and its more formal cousin, mediation, have become recognized professions. People go through special training to become facilitators, and as in all professions, the good ones are very good at what they do. Depending on the task that's in front of you, you may well want to seek this kind of professional assistance for your group. In chapter 3, we talk about the cost of hiring a professional neutral and how such costs should be covered.

There are circumstances in which a professional facilitator is not needed in the convening or assessment phase, although in most of these cases you still need some sort of neutral help from someone who is not a party. Remember that "neutrality" is really in the eyes of the beholders. Suppose there's a relatively small group that's been operating for several years and finds itself unable to move forward. The head of the group—who by all accounts is not the source of the problem— is retiring. It's conceivable that this outgoing head could serve effectively as a neutral party, and "map" a new problem that the group needs to deal with. But note that in this case, the interested parties are already more or less at the table, and the convening challenge is a relatively small one.

Assigning Roles and Responsibilities

Let's assume that one way or another you've talked to or invited the right people, and they've agreed to participate in one way or another. Or, in many cases, you are just confronted with a group that has self-selected or been assigned by someone higher up in the organization. Now what?

Now the people at the table have to (1) agree upon the ground rules that will govern their problem-solving process and (2) define the kinds of responsibilities that they are each willing to accept. We summarize this phase as "signing on." Sample ground rules that might provide a good starting point for almost any kind of group meeting are included in appendix B.

Some of the signing-on issues have to do with group responsibilities. Who's going to facilitate? Who is going to draft the ground rules for the group to consider? What's the scope of the effort (which is sometimes captured in a mission statement)? What's the timetable? If technical advice is needed, where is that going to come from? Who's going to pay for what? What's the overall budget? Who's going to commit what amount of time to the effort? Who's going to keep track of the key points of agreement and disagreement that come out of the discussion?

Other issues have to do with individual responsibilities. The people at the table are there because they represent something. Well, how literally do we mean that? For example, is Joe at the table simply because he seems typical of the people who live in the Mill Pond Road neighborhood immediately adjacent to the high school football field, and who generally have strong feelings about the proposed lighting of that field for night games? Is Joe in some way authorized to speak for that neighborhood? Is he willing and able to take ideas back to his neighbors and get a good reading on their reactions?

What if Joe can't come to a particular meeting? Does he have— should he have—an "alter ego," so that Mill Pond Road doesn't feel left out? Should both Joe and his alter ego attend every meeting?

In a sense, it's all about defining roles and getting everybody at the table to agree to those roles. They have to agree on the role of the group and also on their own roles within the group. They have to agree to a common definition of "representation," and then act according to that definition.

A lot of this depends on the size of your group, and the scope of the issue or problem that your group is trying to address, but even if your group is small and your challenge seems manageable, it makes sense for you to look through the ideas listed and think about which ones pertain to you. Would you benefit from a clearer mission statement, for example? How about a timetable? (If you don't have an external deadline, it's often very helpful to impose an internal one.) Presumably, there is a range of possible actions you can take. Who's going to keep track of what you've looked at, what you decided, and how you got to that decision?

If your decision ever gets challenged—and a surprising number of decisions do get challenged, out there in the world—you're going to be happy that you have that kind of record of all your good work.

Group Problem Solving

Although the next two phases—group problem solving and reaching agreement—inevitably blend into each other, we'll describe them as if they are separate.

We've already talked about the dynamic at most meetings, where—according to Robert's Rules—the proponent of a certain action puts his or her idea forward and looks for an up-or-down vote on that idea. Maybe he or she speaks in favor of the idea. Maybe other people in the room speak for or against it. Maybe there are even a few amendments or improvements offered around the margins of the idea. (In a formal town meeting, significant changes are likely to be ruled "beyond the scope" of the original motion.)

Among the many problems with this approach is the fact that no one is taking responsibility for coming up with proposals that are substantially better for everyone, in the sense of making larger numbers of people more comfortable with them. The whole field of "mutual-gain negotiation" (informally known as "win-win" negotiation) assumes that if people put their minds to it, they can almost always come up with trades that produce a "package deal," which is better for everybody.

The goal of problem solving, in a consensus-building context, is to generate packages, proposals, and ideas that can help all the parties do better than they would in the absence of an agreement. Typically, this happens in several steps. The first might be described as "venting": each party is asked to state any concerns that it may have about other parties, or about what has gone on up to that point. The next step is a round of statements (describing interests or priority concerns) by the various individuals or group representatives. And finally, there's a period of what has been called "inventing." People take what they've heard about each other's interests and try to come up with packages that meet everybody's needs. In general, these various packages are produced in a written form (sometimes called a "single text"). They often include a restatement of the reasons that each party has put forward to explain why it is committed to a particular course of action.

The point of such brainstorming is to keep multiple options alive, so that a full range of combinations can be "tried on for size." Again, the contrast is with Robert's Rules or majority rule in general, in which motions (1) have to be voted up or down, one at a time, and (2) can't be revisited except under extraordinary circumstances.

Sometimes this step in CBA requires multiple sessions. People may need extra time to figure out the relative attractiveness of various packages. Sometimes people need time to discuss the various packages with the people whom they've agreed to represent. Such efforts can only work if everyone agrees to put off making commitments until the group has gone as far as it can in considering options. Thus, the most effective deliberations are those that involve what has been dubbed "inventing without committing."

The facilitator's role varies, depending on the needs of the particular group. In some cases, the facilitator mainly keeps the conversation on track. (If the group is large enough, and involves subgroups responsible for generating ideas across a range of issues, process management can be a complicated job.) In other cases, especially if the parties find themselves stuck—out of options, with nothing much left on the table to trade—the facilitator may get involved by suggesting radically different proposals for consideration by the group. Some hints on being a good facilitator, in case you should ever be assigned that task, are included in appendix B.

Reaching Agreement

The key point here is that in CBA, deciding does not mean voting. Instead, it means **agreeing to agree**.

Whether the facilitator has focused mainly on keeping the conversation on track up to this point, or has been involved in putting together packages for consideration, he or she is in close enough touch with the group to know when the participants are approaching consensus. And here's where the clearly established ground rules from the "signing on" phase can become extremely important. In most cases, the facilitator delivers to the group a statement something like the following: "O.K. Let me summarize where we are. Can everybody live with the following proposal?"

The members of the group know the rules. After hearing the proposal, they are expected to say yes or no. In both cases—but particularly in the case of somebody saying no—they are asked to explain their position. (This is something that never happens when a group is operating under Robert's Rules.) The goal in CBA is to get people to be very clear about their reasons for liking or not liking the package. Here, again, a skilled facilitator earns her keep. She asks the people who are objecting what specific changes they require to make the package acceptable to them (i.e., better for them than no agreement). But beyond that, she may ask questions to shed even more light on where they stand. "Why is it," she might ask, "that among all these people at the table, you're the only one who doesn't like this package? What isn't the group understanding about your concerns?"

The point is not to put people on the spot. In fact, it's just the opposite. Unlike majority rule, the point throughout CBA—and certainly in the deciding phase—is to build effective communications and positive relationships among the parties. People have to be willing to say what's on their minds, though, even if it's unpopular with the rest of the group. The larger group has to be willing to listen hard and respond to the concerns of the unhappy party, usually by trying to invent some modification that will bring them on board.

When the stakes are high, and emotions are in play, skilled facilitation is invaluable. A skilled facilitator disciplines the ways in which people express their disagreements. The facilitator keeps people from saying things in the heat of the moment that might slow down, or even thwart, the effort to reach a consensus.

Holding People to Their Commitments

The final phase in CBA is implementation. Lots of people assume that once the decision is made, the group gets to pack up and go home. Not true! In some ways, the hardest work is yet to be done.

Implementation usually takes time and effort . . . and some times even money. As time passes, things change. People watching the early stages of implementation but who weren't involved in the consensus-building process start to question how *this* particular solution got OK'd. When people start to see real money being spent, especially real public money, they get focused on things in a new way.

In the real world, surprises are inevitable. New people arrive on the scene. The political or economic context changes. A new law makes something possible or impossible. Someone points out that a new technology makes the agreed-upon package a less-than-optimal solution and suggests that the package be revisited.

A good package builds in two contradictory ingredients. One is a strong commitment on the part of the participating parties to stick with what they have promised, often over an extended period of time. The second ingredient is some mechanism for anticipating and dealing with the unanticipated.

In cases where the "wild cards" can be anticipated, it's possible to include contingencies in the package: If X happens, we agree to do so-and-so, but, if Y happens, we agree to do such-and-such. When X or Y actually happens, the group doesn't need to reconvene; the implementing body simply follows the prescribed path.

In most cases, however, the unexpected is going to remain just that: unexpected. The package therefore needs to add up to what we usually call a "nearly self-enforcing agreement." Note the combination of tight (self-enforcing) and loose (nearly) language. Make it as tight and tough as possible, extracting the maximum commitment from all the participants, but also leave the wriggle room necessary to come back and make the agreement even smarter, if necessary.

How is CBA different from majority rule?

Now that you've gotten a feel for the philosophical underpinnings and the mechanics of CBA, let's take a minute to contrast this process with the "majority rule" approach described in chapter 1, which is often governed by Robert's Rules.

The first major difference between CBA and majority rule is the way ideas are put forward. In majority rule, any member of the body can put forward almost any idea he or she wants, as long as he or she follows Robert's Rules. (In some cases, motions are not accepted unless they are presented in writing in advance, through a moderator, or are included in a preprinted agenda.) The sponsor of a motion is not asked the reason behind it, although he or she may choose to speak in support of it. It's relatively hard to change a motion once it is introduced. Amendments (even so-called friendly amendments) may be perceived as hostile or counterproductive by the original sponsor of the motion, who is then likely to oppose them, again without necessarily saying *why*. And although there may be debate—even passionate, far-ranging debate—about the subject at hand, the members of the group are essentially asked to vote the original idea (or perhaps a slightly amended version) up or down.

Henry Ford once told his customers they could have any color car they wanted, as long as it was black. Majority rule (as structured by Robert's Rules) has the same kind of rigidity. The motion is more or less a given; the deliberations are triggered by that motion and largely stay within its boundaries. If someone tries to amend the motion in some significant way, there's a good chance that such an amendment will be ruled "beyond the scope" of the original motion.

There is no incentive in the process to put forward motions that will win support of more than the magical 51 percent. Conversely, there's nothing to prevent somebody from putting forward a blizzard of motions, all done up in procedurally correct ways, which everyone knows have absolutely no chance of passing. Sometimes this happens because the sponsor wants to make a symbolic point. ("Stop the war!" "Bike paths are the future!") Sometimes "it's all about me": I like the sound of my own voice; I like seeing myself on the reruns of the local cable show; I like having people stop me in the supermarket and encourage me to "give 'em hell!"

In other words, the content of the motion often gives way to tactics, or ego, or other things that have little to do with actual problem solving.

CBA is very different. In consensus building, the "motion" (1) takes the form of a statement or proposal that in many cases is framed by the person responsible for helping the group reach agreement, and (2) is formulated in a way that is designed to bring as many people as possible on board. The process manager or facilitator has been in on the deliberations; now he or she comes up with a proposal or package that reflects all of that debate and the concerns that have been expressed throughout.

We've already alluded to the second big difference between CBA and majority rule, which is the vote. Majority rule presupposes an up-or-down vote on a proposal, again with no explanations required or expected. (By the way, note all these junctures in majority rule where "reasons why" are not required.) Consensus building, by contrast, almost never involves voting. It involves dialogue and deliberation that lead to cumulative proposals put forward by the facilitator or a group leader. The arrival of such proposals, which almost never comes as a surprise, prompts a whole new round of discussion: Can you live with this? If not, what would you change so that you *can* live with it?

This is the third major difference between consensus and majority rule: people engaging in CBA have a positive obligation to *improve* the package that is put on the table, if they don't like it. The disaffected person doesn't have the luxury of just sitting around being disaffected.

If that person is unhappy, then he or she has to come up with proposed modifications that will make the package go from unacceptable
to acceptable—not just for them but for everyone in the group.

For example: a facilitator is helping a local citizen task force en-
gaged in updating the local signage bylaws, which govern how businesses can advertise themselves in the community. Most of the
members of the task force, which consists mainly of downtown lawyers and local merchants, like the draft that the group leader has put
before them. But there's one notable exception. A woman who owns a
home adjacent to the business district announces that she believes that
the five-person review board (which will approve or disapprove proposed signs) is likely to be dominated by the local retail community.
The group leader asks her how she would change the draft to address
her concern. Because she understands the process, she has come prepared. Reserving one seat on the five-person board for an architect or
graphic designer, she says, would satisfy her objections. This idea is
added to the mix of ideas on the table for review and discussion by the
entire task force.

To summarize: under Robert's Rules, you put finished motions on
the table, then you debate them in a process that works against significant alterations, and then you vote them up or down. In consensus
building, you put lots of ideas and interests on the table (prior to anyone making any firm commitments), debate those ideas and interests,
and *then* a group leader or a neutral facilitator formulates a package
designed to meet all the interests of everyone involved to the greatest
extent possible. This, in turn, generates more ideas. If there's a vote at
the end of the process, it's mainly to acknowledge the "overwhelming
agreement" that has been reached.

Three leadership models

The matter of group leadership could have been included in the previous section on the differences between CBA and majority rule, but it's
important enough that we wanted to call it out on its own. These two

processes demand very different kinds of things from their respective group leaders. We can describe three models of leadership, which sit on a spectrum from majority rule (Robert's Rules) to CBA.

In majority rule, the assumption—either stated or unstated—is that the leader's role is to take personal responsibility for the group's success. The leader sets the agenda for the meeting. The leader tends to formulate the motion and puts it in front of the group, sometimes directly and sometimes through a handpicked proxy. The assumptions behind this approach are that (1) the leader can somehow stretch her thinking to figure out what everybody else at the table wants, and (2) that she can come up with a proposal that will be in the best interests of the assembly as a whole. We are especially used to seeing this approach to group leadership in business settings.

It's not too much to say that in majority-rule situations, **we cast the leader as the savior of the group**. He gets the group together, establishes a formal or informal hierarchy within the group (with him at the top, of course), sets the agenda, comes up with a solution, and assembles enough support for that solution—51 percent, or maybe more—to get it approved by a vote. He's the person who comes to the table with some personal clout, and doesn't hesitate to use it to exert pressure on the other participants as necessary.

The implicit assumption in this model of leadership is that the group is not capable of arriving at a good solution on its own: it needs a strong personality to serve as its shepherd. The shepherd uses her influence to extract compromises from the other members of the group and thereby saves them from themselves.

Needless to say, this is a lot of responsibility to put on the leader's shoulders. The pool of people willing and able to serve as "leaders" of this type is fairly small. That's why in a business or community organization, you tend to see the same faces over and over again. It's also why you tend to get leaders who are accustomed to getting their way, often by simply steamrolling the people who appear to be obstacles to that end. They tend to be very aggressive. They are prone to say things like, "You can't make an omelet without breaking eggs." Or, "If you can't take the heat, stay out of the kitchen."

The second model on our spectrum of leadership is the **leader as process manager**. This model assumes that with the right amount of procedural support from the leader, the group will get its work done.

The classic example here is the moderator at a New England town meeting. The moderator is exclusively a process person, or at least she tries to be. She keeps order. She reminds everybody of the rules. In some cases, the moderator may have a parliamentarian helping her with the more obscure aspects of Robert's Rules, but she's generally expected to be enough of a procedural expert to keep the meeting on track. She is also expected to be a forceful enough personality to be able to "ride herd" on the group when it starts to get rowdy.

The process manager, like the savior, is definitely protecting the group from itself. Instead of throwing substantive life preservers, like a lifeguard, she throws procedural life preservers. The assumption, again, is that the group is not capable of performing effectively on its own.

To switch metaphors: Picture the lion-tamer at the circus. If he's not there with his whip, keeping the lions up on their stools, what's likely to happen? Chaos! Somebody has to be there, on the alert, cracking the whip.

Like the lions up on the stools, the group invests authority in the process manager. (This is reinforced by the dominant style that is usually exhibited by the process manager.) And, by extension, the group invests authority in the *process*: if we just pay scrupulous attention to the process, we'll get to a good solution.

This, as we've already seen, is an illusion. The better the process manager is at playing by Robert's Rules, the harder it is to get good ideas on the table, to build consensus around those ideas, and to implement a solution effectively.

Which brings us to the third model of leadership: **facilitative leadership**, in which the leader serves mainly as the convener of the process. This is the model used in CBA, and it is at the far end of the spectrum from the leader as savior, shepherd, or lifeguard.

This kind of leader focuses almost entirely on getting the right people to the table, or at least getting their ideas represented in some meaningful way. The leader-as-convener gets the process going, and then steps back and lets the group take responsibility for finding the right solution.

If your head is full of traditional visions of leadership, you may by astonished at this notion. Let the *group* take responsibility? Isn't that like letting the sheep run away, or the swimmers drown, or the lions jump down off their stools?

Of course not. We've already introduced the additional role of the facilitator. This person can be a skilled technician or someone selected by the group (and seen as neutral) who can take responsibility for managing the process. The members of the group work with the facilitator to establish procedural ground rules, and then use those rules to generate a shared solution. Keep in mind that these ground rules are the group's own invention, which in most cases means that the members of the group are more likely to honor them, in spirit and letter, than they are to honor someone else's rules. They *own* the process, and therefore, they're less likely to abuse it. At the same time, once they have their own rules in place, they're more likely to focus on issues of *substance*.

One way to contrast these three leadership models is to ask the question, where is the creativity?

In the leader-as-savior model, obviously, the creativity resides almost entirely in the leader. This leader is the be-all and end-all. In the process-manager model, the creativity resides in the artful enforcement of a set of rules (and to some extent, in the rules themselves). In the facilitative leadership model, the creativity is presumed to reside in the group. The leader, and the rules, are simply tools for getting the right group working effectively on the right problem in a constructive fashion.

We know which model General Robert endorsed. Based on what you've read so far, which model do *you* want to bet on?

Revisiting the soccer league

Think back to the first incident described in our introduction, in which a group of parents decides to try and get rid of a coach who has gotten into a (profane) shouting match with one of them.

Let's review the circumstances in which the president of that league found himself, in the days leading up to the dramatic emergency meeting:

- The group has no effective leadership. Leadership jobs in the league are thankless tasks, and the league's president, vice president, and treasurer tend to be chosen by means of the "short straw."
- The membership of the group is not well defined. In the past, voting privileges have been extended to just about anybody who showed up at a given meeting.
- Some people are convinced that at one time the league adopted written bylaws, but no one can find a copy. Apparently, the by-laws stated that the group would follow *Robert's Rules of Order*.
- The facts of the original shouting match are still in question—at least, up to the point when the referee stepped in and ended the game.
- At the "emergency meeting," tempers are running high. One faction is eager to *take a vote*, most likely because that group believes that they can get the result they want.
- At the climactic moment, the coach himself walks into the room, and—in a dramatic flourish—threatens to sue.

The best you can say about these circumstances is that the coach and his lawyer may have done the crowd a huge favor. If they have broken the momentum toward judgment, that is, if they have defused the "lynch mob" mentality, they may have created an opening for consensus building to occur.

What should the soccer league do now? Let's review the six foundations of CBA, and suggest some specifics:

1. **In any group or organizational effort to make decisions, it is crucial to clarify the responsibilities of the people involved to others they are presumed to speak for, or otherwise represent.**
The soccer league has to figure out who will speak for whom, and how. Who are the contending groups, and how will they be represented?

2. **Once a group gets together, it should not start work until its members clarify what their mission is, what their agenda will include (and not include), and what the ground rules are that will guide their conversations.**
The league has to straighten out its leadership and governing structure. It needs to find and understand its bylaws. It needs to decide whether it will limit the scope of its efforts to this one case—the coach in question—or to broader issues of hiring, firing, and so on. It needs to define how these discussions will be conducted, so that people can disagree without being disagreeable.

3. **Before the members of a group try to make decisions on anything, they should engage in joint fact-finding.**
It would be very helpful to have all parties agree on a set of facts regarding the incident in question. It might also be helpful to investigate how other leagues address these kinds of issues. If legal actions are a concern, the group should find out exactly what it can and can't do.

4. **Groups should try to generate agreements that leave everyone better off than they would have been if no agreement had been reached.**
The question is, how can the league broaden the range of issues on the table so that the outcome won't simply be a win/lose? (The coach stays; the coach goes.) Is there a deal that could be struck between the two aggrieved parties that would satisfy them both? Is there a set of "going-forward" rules that, if adopted, would make all parties feel like something good had come out of the conflict?

5. **It is important to hold people working in groups responsible for taking a written version of a draft agreement back to the people or groups whom they represent.**

The people involved in the discussions have to be prepared to go back to the groups they represent, explain the process, and explain why the result is the best possible outcome.

6. **Groups should always think ahead about the things that can go wrong, as they try to implement whatever decisions or agreements they reach.**

The people involved in the discussions have to figure out who might object to the proposed deal, and why. Is there a regional, state, or national soccer organization that might claim some sort of jurisdiction? Is there any chance that someone who hasn't been involved will take legal action anyway? How should next year's schedule be adjusted to minimize the chance of accidental confrontations, and maximize the "healing" period?

Now let's get back to *your* meeting. If you're in a situation like the president of our fictitious soccer league, the first thing you should do is find your bylaws and figure out whether your meetings are subject to Robert's Rules.

If they are, your group will have to decide what to do about that. In some cases, groups simply ignore that fact and try to do their business informally, in a less rule-driven way. The problem with that strategy is that someone may try to hold you to your own rules. Is there a lawyer on your board? This person may point out (accurately) that if your articles of incorporation cite Robert's Rules as your procedural guide, then you have a legal obligation to follow those rules. Worse yet, someone may show up at your first meeting—or your second or third meeting—and insist on playing by those rules. If he or she is steeped in Robert's Rules and no one else is, you will have a problem.

One solution is to use *Robert's Rules* to suspend Robert's Rules. (Parliamentarians may object; it's worth sounding out a few people in advance of such a move.) Once the group's consensus building efforts are complete, you can reinstate the parliamentary process. Or, if it's not too onerous, simply take the steps necessary to change your bylaws and do away with Robert's Rules. (You can adopt the CBA procedures outlined in part 2 of this book instead!) One school committee that we worked with simply followed its normal policy-review process (i.e., first reading at meeting A, second reading and a vote at meeting B) to get rid of Robert's Rules entirely, thereby opening the door to consensus building.

On to the specifics

In this chapter, we've tried to present a snapshot of consensus building. As a group, you convene, sort out responsibilities, engage in problem solving, clarify the consensus you have reached, and then implement it. You try hard to make the original agreement stick, and under circumstances agreed upon in advance, you reconvene to make the original agreement conform to any changes or unanticipated events.

Maybe this still strikes you as too complicated: mission statements, outside helpers, money, lots of back and forth among the concerned parties, packages in writing, and so on. Maybe you're tempted to side with General Robert, at this point: make sure you've got 51 percent or better, put your best idea on the table, get your yes vote . . . and try to get out of the meeting alive.

Stick with us. CBA is (sometimes) about going slowly at first in order to reduce the overall amount of time it takes to reach an agreement that satisfies everyone and that actually sticks. As you read the following chapters, which dig deeper into each phase of CBA, and which track the experiences of the imaginary Blaine Bicentennial Committee, keep thinking about the *end-to-end* consequence of siding with General Robert. How will you feel when at the next majority-rule session, some group surprises you with its own 51 percent and undoes your previous triumph? What's your next move going to be? Sway a vote, get back your majority, and throw the engines into reverse again?

Wouldn't it be better—and take less time, end to end—to get it right the first time, and have the results stick?

Key Terms Explained in Chapter 2
(For further clarification, see Part 2:
The Five Essential Steps in the
Consensus Building Approach, page 167)

Consensus
Informed agreement
Philosophical foundations of consensus building
The five-step model
Convening
The convener
Assessment
Assigning roles and responsibilities
Representation
Facilitation
Neutrality
Facilitating group problem solving
Ground rules
✓ Mutual gains negotiation
✓ Venting
Inventing without committing
Single-text procedure
Reaching agreement
Alternatives to voting
Holding people to their commitments
Nearly self-enforcing agreements
✓ Contingent agreements
Three models of group leadership
The leader as savior
The leader as process manager
✓ Facilitative leadership
Using CBA in a Robert's Rules environment

3

~

Getting the Right People
to the Table

Getting Started

The first step in consensus building is **convening**. The point of convening is to give the potential parties a chance to help decide who
needs to be involved, and whether and how to move ahead.

In this absolutely critical phase of the process, somebody has to
determine whether the minimum conditions for a successful CBA effort can be met. If not, the group may have to revert to majority rule,
hold its nose, and take a vote.

Somebody has to perform an assessment of the conflict or issue at
hand. Based on that assessment, somebody has to figure out (1) who
needs to be consulted or brought to the table, and (2) how to get them
there. At the same time, somebody has to begin the process of securing
the resources that will be needed to conduct a full-fledged consensus-
building process. By "resources," we mean both human and financial
resources. And finally, somebody has to make a judgment about
whether to use CBA.

We will cover all these topics in this chapter. But first, let's look at this
"somebody" who is doing, or helping to do, all these important things.

Identifying the convener

Not surprisingly, the "somebody" who runs a convening effort is referred to as the **convener**. This person plays a critical start-up role in the process. First of all, without a convener, the process either doesn't get off the ground at all, or doesn't get very far. In some instances, there might actually be multiple conveners. For example, several agencies or officials with formal responsibility might co-convene a consultative process.

Second, the convener needs to be **someone who knows the "movers and shakers"** on the particular issue, that is, the people who represent key points of view or interests and whose influence can make or break any possible negotiated agreement. The convener also has to be someone who has some stature in the affected organization, company, or community. In other words, when the convener sends an e-mail to or leaves a phone message for one of those movers and shakers, he has to have enough clout or goodwill to get a reply.

Third, the convener has to be seen as **reasonably fair-minded**. If there are already armed camps on both sides of an issue, it's difficult for a high-profile member of one of these camps to play the convener's role (although in a corporate context, where hierarchies are powerful, this often happens).

And finally, it's very helpful if the convener has **some understanding of basic consensus-building techniques**, and how CBA differs from traditional majority-rule procedures. This will help the convener avoid process mistakes and equip him or her with convincing arguments to use when somebody wonders why the group doesn't just follow Robert's Rules.

The mayor asks for help

In chapter 1, we promised you a concrete illustration of CBA in the context of a new group, so that you could get a sense of how it actually works in a from-the-ground-up situation. So now, let's get that scenario going.

Imagine a town in the mid-Atlantic region of the United States that is approaching the two-hundredth anniversary of its founding. The town meeting has voted to mount a bicentennial celebration—a seemingly simple task. We say "seemingly" because throwing a birthday party for a town is actually a lot more complicated than it might seem and, like many other issues in the public arena, turns out to be loaded with economic, cultural, and emotional issues. We'll call our town "Blaine," in honor of the town in the film *Waiting for Guffman*, which depicted a group of earnest citizens facing a similar challenge.

The mayor of Blaine—we'll call him "Mike"—has been procrastinating about dealing with the bicentennial. Mike likes a party as much as anyone, but there always seems to be something more pressing on his plate. In addition, the town's finance committee has allocated only $5,000 for the event. That's a lot of money for Blaine, but as Mike knows, not a lot of money for a town-wide celebration that may stretch over several days. The event is now less than a year away, and Mike realizes that he has to *do* something. He calls his friend and longtime supporter Bill, and asks if Bill can stop by the town hall later in the day. Bill agrees to a brief meeting at 3:00 p.m. on his way to the airport.

Bill runs the largest factory in town. He built the company, an old family business, back up from almost nothing, and he now employs several hundred people. He is known as a smart, tough, demanding boss and is rumored to be one of the wealthiest people in Blaine. He has backed Mike in each of his three successful runs for mayor.

Bill arrives slightly ahead of schedule, and is shown into Mike's office immediately. After some friendly banter, the mayor gets to the point:

MIKE: Bill, I need a big favor. I need you to head up a committee for the town's bicentennial. It's coming up in June, and I'm a little behind the eight ball.

BILL: I remember hearing something about this. What's involved?

MIKE: In a nutshell, town meeting authorized the creation of a bicentennial committee last year with the members to be named by me. So as far as I'm concerned, somebody has to pull together a blue-ribbon group, come up with a plan and a budget, and basically make it happen. And since the town can only kick in $5,000, I'm sure we're going to need some private fund-raising to close the gap.

BILL: Doesn't sound too tough. Is there anybody out there with any experience with this kind of stuff?

MIKE: Well, I think that the head of the Youth Department—her name is Connie—did something like this in the last town she worked in. Same kind of thing for the community college there. I don't know the details. And of course, you'll need to get the Historical Commission involved. My assistant has a folder with a couple of letters in it from people who have volunteered to do one thing or another. But I think it's mostly a case of touching the right bases, making the right people feel involved, and coming up with something that we can all be proud of. You know . . . our two-hundredth birthday, and all.

BILL: Happy to take it on for you, Mike. I'll make some calls and get back to you with some names, probably starting with this Connie person. And I'll ask my secretary to keep your office in the loop as things develop.

So the Blaine Bicentennial Committee gets its first member: Bill. Bill is the top name on Mike's list of usual suspects, and for good reason. He's a hard-working, results-oriented kind of guy, who gets tapped to lead all kinds of things in Blaine and almost always delivers the goods. After Bill leaves his office, Mike lets out a sigh of relief. One less thing to worry about! He has successfully handed off the convening responsibility to Bill.

Meeting the minimum conditions

One common mistake is failing to invest enough time in the front end of such a process, that is, finding allies, sniffing out possibilities, and laying the groundwork for consensus building. Most people aren't used to "going slow to go fast." Take a CEO like Bill. Bill is accustomed to calling together his operating group, discussing an issue, and making a decision—often on the spot. This is possible because he controls the context in which decision making happens; he sets the rules and has the power to implement any decision.

CBA is different. In consensus building, you have to meet certain minimum conditions before you can even get off the ground. At the outset, the convener has to initiate a dialogue with at least some of the key players. Using the assessment process described on pages 46–49, the convener needs to gauge whether these players are open to the idea of working together and, ideally, serve as an effective advocate for this approach. He has to get a sense of whether these key people think there is room to create options and invent a mutually advantageous solution.

Some issues don't lend themselves to consensus building because they deal with what we call fundamental beliefs. They are simply too "hot" and too closely linked to people's sense of their own identity. To cite an extreme example: abortion rights is usually a non-negotiable issue for people on both sides. But you may be surprised at the range of issues that people think are non-negotiable. Some people are fundamentally hostile, for example, to building a much-needed athletic field in a town-owned forest *under any circumstances*, and they simply aren't open to other views. (They hate to see trees cut down, their property abuts the site, or whatever.) Sometimes, though, non-negotiable items are open to discussion once people realize they are not being asked to compromise. Instead, they are being asked to consider different questions, different ways of reframing the initial issue.

At the other end of the spectrum, some issues don't generate enough interest to sustain a consensus building effort. The truth is, consensus building takes time and commitment. It requires participants who feel that something important is at stake. An issue that is too "small" is likely to be met with apathy.

In our experience, though, it's usually not apathy that keeps people out of these kinds of processes. More often, people stay away because they don't believe that anyone will listen to them, they are afraid they don't know enough about the questions at hand to make much of a contribution, or they think that group efforts to solve problems tend to be unproductive.

CBA is all about listening to people, helping people understand an issue well enough to invent a good solution, and then *implementing that solution.* The convener has to find a core group with a sufficient commitment who are open to creative problem solving.

As you can see, meeting the minimum conditions very much depends on the specifics of the issue at hand. In general, the goal of this initial step is to assemble a reasonably diverse core of people who are committed to defining the issue accurately, and in ways that keep lots of options open, and to expand their ranks as necessary to make a successful consensus-building process possible.

Performing the assessment

In order to get the convening process off the ground, someone has to write an *assessment*—a simple, descriptive summary of the views of the stakeholders. (In cases where a conflict has already emerged, it may be called a "conflict assessment.") The assessment usually emerges from a series of one-on-one, "not for attribution" interviews or conversations.

Who does this? In some cases, the convener and the assessor can be the same person. In other cases—because of the complexity of the issue, or because there is no person qualified and willing to serve both roles—the assessor is a second person, generally brought in by the convener with the approval of others involved in the early stages. There are good reasons that many conveners decide to hand over the assessment and related tasks to another individual.

What does an assessment look like? In complicated cases, the assessment may run many pages and include exhibits and appendices. In other cases, the assessment may be a single short paragraph. For example:

> Some of the members of the Smith School Parent-Teacher Association have proposed that the PTA formally vote to endorse the school-improvement bond issue being put before the town's voters in the November election. Other members, while supporting improved schools, believe that the PTA should not involve itself in political issues. Some members of this second

group believe that this kind of involvement is prohibited either by federal laws governing charitable organizations or by the PTA's charter. Most parties agree that the outcome of the November vote is extremely important to the future of education at the Smith School. Because the group's last pre-election meeting is in the last week of October, this issue needs to be resolved before that meeting.

It takes only a few minutes to write an assessment like the preceding paragraph. In real life, though, getting to a statement like this would most likely reflect a lot of work on the part of the assessor. It would summarize perhaps a dozen conversations and reflect several rounds of edits by all the involved parties. It might still be only a working draft to be shared again—maybe several times—with potential participants before the final decision as to whether to proceed with a consensus building effort is made.

Information gathered during this phase usually proves very valuable to the convener in completing subsequent phases of the convening process. The act of generating the assessment also helps potential participants in the process by crystallizing the real issue in their minds and introducing them to the mechanics of CBA.

Earlier, we mentioned the importance of *neutrality* on the part of the assessor. Especially in the assessment phase, the convener and the assessor have to avoid advocacy in any form. An assessment with a built-in bias will not only fail to address the conflict adequately, it also will antagonize and possibly drive potential participants away.

Confidentiality is also critically important. Assessment involves a process of exploration; therefore, it needs to be informal, flexible, and completely off-the-record. When the assessor approaches someone, she usually says something along the lines of, "I'm happy to have the opportunity to talk with you about Project X. I'm going to summarize what I learn from you as part of the assessment I'm preparing. But nothing that you tell me will be attributed to you personally."

The assessor is not responsible for providing a blow-by-blow account of who feels which way about each aspect of Project X. Instead, she uses the evolving assessment document to decide whether CBA is the right way to proceed in this instance, and who the key stakeholders are.

Contrast this with a process governed by Robert's Rules, where one expects the formal minutes of a committee to include details about who proposed, and who opposed, a certain course of action. The minutes are also likely to include "pro" and "con" positions, often attributed to individuals. This kind of attribution tends to polarize a debate and lock people into opposing positions. Politicians, in particular, don't like to be accused of waffling or "flip-flopping." Once they stake out a position publicly, they generally feel compelled to stick with it. Therefore, simple statements of a point of view often give way to posturing and exaggeration. Opening statements become permanent positions.

In some cases, while preparing the assessment, the assessor will find it helpful to prepare a simple grid summarizing the situation in chart form. One axis of the chart lists key issues; the other lists key players or groups. The assessor fills in the boxes that result to indicate how important a particular issue is to a particular player.

In chapter 2, we gave the example of an effort to revise a town's signage bylaw. The grid that mapped that issue might look as follows, using a system of 1 to 5 checkmarks to indicate the intensity of concern felt by the key players:

SIGNAGE BYLAW ASSESSMENT

Key players	Helping commerce	Aesthetics	Real estate values	Tax receipts	Safety
		Key Issues			
Local merchants (nonresident)	✓✓✓✓✓	✓✓	✓	✓	✓
Local merchants (resident)	✓✓✓✓✓	✓✓✓✓	✓✓✓	✓✓	✓
Residents (non-merchant)	✓✓	✓✓✓✓✓	✓✓✓✓✓	✓✓✓	✓
Elected officials	✓✓✓	✓✓✓	✓✓✓	✓✓✓✓	✓✓✓
Real estate firms	✓✓✓	✓✓✓	✓✓✓✓✓	✓	✓
Public safety officials	✓	✓	✓	✓	✓✓✓✓✓

Of course, this is only a tool, intended to help the assessor graphically portray a preliminary breakdown of issues and potential stakeholders. The assessor may or may not choose to share this grid with the interviewees along the way. In some cases, an interviewee may respond to the grid by suggesting additional players or issues that ought to be included, or by indicating that the weighting of a particular topic seems inaccurate. The assessor is free to decide how (or whether) to factor those opinions into the next version of the grid.

In addition to depicting the key players and issues, the assessment ultimately is used to generate a project work plan, in which the assessor evaluates how much time will be needed for the dialogue, and what kinds of resources (financial and otherwise) will be required. Like the depiction of the central issue, this work plan begins as a very general statement and becomes increasingly specific as more information becomes available. We will return to the project work plan shortly.

Identifying the right people

CBA, as noted at the beginning of this chapter, involves getting the right people to the table. In many cases, this happens in steps—one step at a time—as different circles of individuals become involved.

The **first circle** tends to include the movers and shakers mentioned earlier: the people who have already made it clear that they have a stake in the outcome of the discussion. They may have the power to block a particular decision. They may have too high a profile in the community to be ignored. Or, they may have some expertise that is especially relevant. One way or another, though, they are the people who obviously matter when it comes to this issue. Their absence will hurt the process; more positively, their participation may help things move forward.

In talking to this first group, the assessor typically asks, "Who else should I be meeting with?" The answers to this question point toward the **second circle** of potential participants. These people may be one step removed from the initial stages of the debate, but they too may be potential blockers (or strong advocates) of particular solutions.

A **third circle** includes people who aren't directly affected but may be helpful to the successful resolution of the issue. This category might include volunteers who have heard about the issue and believe that they can help resolve it. The assessor may also decide that it's important to include in this circle individuals or groups who aren't in a position to represent themselves. In some discussions of environmental issues, for example, the assessor sometimes takes responsibility for finding someone to represent the interests of "future generations," obviously a group that isn't yet prepared to speak for itself.

Again, this highlights a clear contrast with Robert's Rules, which allocate all aspects of problem definition and decision making to the group that has a formal vote. This leads to a relatively predictable process, of course, but it's one that tends to exclude interested parties and good ideas.

Assembling the resources

CBA always requires hard work by well-meaning people. In some cases, it also requires some financial investment. The convener has to take responsibility for identifying the resources—the people and the dollars—necessary to reach a successful outcome. While the convener is overseeing the assessment (and perhaps preparing the grid), she is also trying to get a handle on the kinds of financial support that may be needed.

In some ways, the people issue is the toughest. As the assessor works through these various circles of people, she keeps an eye out for potential members of a core group who will actually sit at the table and do the problem solving.

Who should be at the table? One key question that the assessor has to think about is *representation*. How effectively can a potential participant represent the interests of a category or group? And—going in the opposite direction—how effectively can that potential participant represent CBA to his "constituents"? In addition, the assessor asks questions such as: Does this individual have the kind of substantive knowledge that we need? Is she open to the idea of a consensus-building process? Does she have the time and will she commit to doing the work?

Sometimes there doesn't appear to be an individual skilled or committed enough to play this role. In such cases, the convener has to look harder! There is almost always someone out there, if the issue at hand is significant.

In other cases, there may be more than one person who seems qualified to fill a certain seat at the table. If so, the assessor has a tough choice to make. One useful approach is for the assessor to list the names of all people who are possible representatives of an identified group or category and to hold that list up against the anticipated *timetable* for the process. Sometimes it becomes clear from looking at things (like vacation plans, business-travel commitments, or other real-world conflicts) that some otherwise qualified people simply can't get involved to the extent necessary. If there is still an oversupply of qualified people in a particular category, the assessor may ask this group to caucus privately and choose its own representative.

In this way, the convener gradually develops a list that consists of "first choices" and alternates. This means that, in effect, each stakeholder group has two identified representatives: a front-line person, and an alternate. If the front-line person has to miss a meeting, the alternate will be there to fill in according to the ground rules agreed upon in advance.

This raises the larger issue of which ground rules will govern the process. Obviously, as the convener and assessor try to secure commitments from potential participants, they have to describe the process that people are being asked to commit to. (The overview provided in chapter 2 can help with this task.) At the same time, the assessor is proposing—and constantly modifying—a set of proposed ground rules. These cover things like how often and where the group will meet, a suggested timetable, and any specific conditions that one or more parties have imposed. Are there clear-cut rules governing conduct at the table? Who will draft agendas and write up a short progress report after each meeting? Will all meetings be face-to-face, or will some be conducted on-line? How do front-line representatives and their alternates work together?

We've already mentioned the project work plan. While the assessor is identifying the team that will sit at the table, he or she is also noting the resources that may be needed. The term "consensus building" covers a great range of activities. By extension, the convening function can range from modest to enormous. On one end of the spectrum is a small effort—say, twenty phone calls or e-mail exchanges and some follow-up conversations. The consensus-building process that grows out of this kind of convening can almost certainly be handled by volunteers. In fact, the majority of consensus-building processes that take place every day in business firms, local governments, and community organizations are ad hoc efforts staffed by volunteers.

By way of contrast, we have been involved in preparing assessments at the global scale. In advance of the Kyoto Climate Change negotiations, for instance, we were asked to help convene a global assembly (of political figures, experts, and advocates) to see if a consensus could be reached on key ideas to include in the formal treaty negotiations. Hundreds of interviews were required. The assessment ultimately led to what is called a "multi-stakeholder dialogue," and that, in turn, produced some of the key elements of what turned out to be a successful global agreement.

As the assessor turns up new information, it may become clear that the issue at hand is far too complicated and involves too many interest groups to be handled on a volunteer basis. When this is the case, the assessor may suggest to the interested parties that they need to hire a professional mediator or facilitator. That means there will be an upfront assessment cost. A case of such complexity may also require additional professional services, for example, meeting planning or report writing, which need to be built into the upfront cost. The good news here is that the bigger the issue, the more places there will be to look for financial support.

If you determine that your issue or conflict requires the services of someone who specializes in providing neutral services, there are plenty of places to go for help. (Check your local phone book. The Association for Conflict Resolution, the American Bar Association's Section on Dispute Resolution, the CPR Institute for Dispute Resolution are all good starting points, and many private firms offer similar services.) Again, the costs of such a service should be built into the project work plan.

As noted above, the project work plan becomes increasingly specific over time as the convener does his or her work. In its final form, the plan should include a clear timetable with key milestones linked to specific dates as much as possible. It should include a budget that is reasonably detailed, with upfront costs indicated, and an idea about how those costs will be met. It should commit to writing any ground rules and other procedural issues that have been agreed to by all parties— unless, of course, the parties have agreed *not* to commit certain things to writing.

The goal, in the convening stage, is to create a structure that is tight enough to allow for the effective conduct of business but also loose enough to allow creative problem solving. When the assessment is finished, there should be a relatively short document (no more than ten to fifteen pages), which has been reviewed by everyone who was interviewed. Based on the material presented, the assessor should be able to make a very specific recommendation to the convener about whether to proceed with a consensus building effort. If the answer is yes, the assessor should also include a detailed list of the people to be invited, a work plan, a budget, and proposed ground rules.

Convening, and reconvening, in Blaine

That's how convening *should* go. Now let's see how it unfolds in Blaine.

If you think back to the scenario that we introduced earlier in this chapter, you'll recall that Mike (the mayor of Blaine) has asked his friend and supporter Bill (the CEO of a large local company) to organize the town's bicentennial celebration. Looking back at the criteria (see Identifying the convener, page 42), it's clear that Bill has three of the four qualifications needed to help Mike convene the process. He knows the movers and shakers. He has stature (the movers and shakers almost certainly will return his phone calls). He's not identified with one approach to bicentennials as opposed to another. (The truth, as Bill readily admits, is that he's never even thought much about bicentennials!) As for the fourth criterion—knowing something about CBA—Bill comes up short on this score.

Three out of four isn't bad. And, as we will see, there are resources available to cover Bill's one shortcoming. Let's tune in to the next conversation between Mike and Bill, which takes place a week after the first one:

MIKE: So how's our party planning going?

BILL: Well, I have to admit, Mike, it's tougher than I anticipated.

MIKE: What's the problem?

BILL: I called a couple of friends who've been helpful in pulling together special events in the past—things out at the club, and so on. They seemed willing enough to sit through some meetings, and maybe kick in some money. But some of those other people you talked about—the Historical Commission types, and those people who wrote you to volunteer their services—just didn't seem interested in helping out. Or maybe they just weren't interested in working with *me*. A couple of them seemed to want all kinds of assurances about this and that before they'd agree to sign up.

MIKE: Like what?

BILL: Well, like this Vince guy from the historic group. He wanted me to promise that we wouldn't "sanitize" everything. I asked him what the hell that meant, and he said that any real celebration of the town's history would have to deal with labor, and unions, and so on. I told him I didn't see having a parade with a bunch of floats celebrating strikers.

MIKE: [*laughs*] Spoken like a true capitalist. OK; I get the picture. Did you get hold of Connie from the Youth Department?

BILL: No. To tell you the truth, I forgot all about her.

MIKE: Give her a call. People say she did great things pulling to-
          gether groups at the community college where she used to
          work. That's one reason we hired her, in fact. I'm sure she
          could free up some time to help you out.

The next day, Bill calls the Youth Department and leaves a message
for Connie. She calls back within the hour, and they agree to meet at
the local coffee shop for lunch. Over sandwiches and coffee, they talk
about the problems Bill is having getting the Blaine Bicentennial Committee off the ground:

BILL: So. That's where it stands. I don't want to let the mayor
          down, but I'm not feeling good about this.

CONNIE: From what I can see, Bill, you're exactly the right guy to
          serve as the overall head of the process. A lot of people
          around town know you and respect you. But you're prob-
          ably *not* the right guy to set the agenda for the committee
          or to make sure that everybody gets heard. In a public pro-
          cess like this, everybody needs to get heard. Believe me!

BILL: I don't see why this has to be so complicated. It's just a
          party, for god's sake. We have a goal, a deadline, and a bud-
          get. We should just jump in there and get the job done.

CONNIE: But you're already finding out it's not working like that,
          right? Some people, like Vince, aren't seeing it the same
          way you do. And those volunteers aren't exactly rushing to
          sign up.

BILL: So what do you suggest?

CONNIE: I'll tell you what. I'll make sure that Mike is OK with me
          putting some hours into this. Meanwhile, you call back the
          people you've already talked to, and tell them that I'm go-
          ing to be helping you with this job, that I want to talk with
          them for a half-hour sometime soon, and that you'd really
          appreciate it if they'd help me out. Once I have your OK,

I'll call them, pick their brains, and come up with a road
map for how the group might move forward.

BILL: Can't hurt, I guess. I'll call them all back, and then I'll have
my assistant e-mail you the contact information.

CONNIE: Great. So let's start with *you*, Bill. And let me assure you
that whatever you say about your hopes for this celebra-
tion will be confidential and will be worked into the road
map I just mentioned.

Bill agrees to this ground rule, saying that he needs regular updates
from Connie and wants a summary of her progress after two weeks,
and then gives Connie her first interview (on which she takes extensive notes). After he gets back to his office, he gets back in touch with
all of the people the mayor originally steered him toward and tells
them that Connie will be calling them. Everyone, even Vince, seems
willing to talk to Connie.

Over the course of the following two weeks, he gets a series of e-
mails from Connie reporting on her progress. She has either met or
talked on the phone with everybody on Bill's original list. She has also
talked to some additional people, some of whose names Bill recog-
nizes and others he doesn't. A couple of people have called Bill and
asked what's going on; he has simply said that he and Connie are trying a new approach and that he'd appreciate their help.

At the end of the two-week period, Bill and Connie get together
again for lunch. Connie explains how she has worked her way out
through several "circles" of stakeholders, gathering insights (and more
names) over the course of her two weeks of conversations. She shows
Bill a draft of what she calls an "assessment," explaining that although
the document will certainly continue to evolve, it's been blessed (on a
provisional basis) by the individuals with whom she has shared it. It
reads as follows:

The town of Blaine will be celebrating its bicentennial in June. Town meeting has authorized an expenditure of $5,000 for that purpose and autho-
rized the creation of a Blaine Bicentennial Committee. It has assigned to

the mayor the task of organizing the celebration. Mike, in turn, has asked Bill to take responsibility for setting up the committee and making sure that its work gets done successfully.

A number of groups have expressed an interest in the celebration. Most interested parties are proud of their town and want to make sure that the celebration reflects that pride. There is substantial disagreement over how best to accomplish that—whether through a parade, a dramatic production, a series of articles in the local newspaper, fireworks displays, a carnival, a special town meeting, cable TV shows, or some combination of the above.

There is also significant disagreement about how history should be used in the celebration. One group (whom I refer to as the "traditionalists") believes that the history component should be exclusively positive: a picture of the past that is entirely positive and progressive. They want to use history solely for *celebration*.

A second group (the "modernists," for our purposes) believes that history should be used for *instruction*. According to this view, Blaine has to acknowledge the contributions of groups (e.g., Native Americans, immigrants, women, etc.) whose role has been ignored in the past. Many in this group feel that a "warts-and-all" approach is called for.

Some individuals have expressed a willingness to contribute money toward the celebration but on condition that the message be "appropriate." (As indicated above, different people define this in different ways.) This is important because the $5,000 appropriation is unlikely to cover the costs of the celebration, no matter what form it takes, and private support is likely to be needed. Several people feel strongly that it would be better to do nothing than to do something "on the cheap" that might reflect badly on Blaine. At the other end of the spectrum are individuals who feel that in a time of fiscal constraints, *no* tax dollars should be spent on the bicentennial.

There are other specific concerns about the celebration. Some people living adjacent to possible celebration sites—the fair grounds, the high school football stadium, likely parade routes, and others—want reassurances that the celebration won't create noise, litter, or traffic problems. The town's public-safety officials are on record as having concerns about fireworks. The school department has informed the mayor that although it supports the bicentennial celebration in principle, it is unwilling to take on any new activities that might divert resources away from the task of educating Blaine's school children.

Connie also hands Bill a copy of a chart, or what she calls a map of stakeholder concerns, that summarizes what she has learned. It reads as follows:

MAP OF STAKEHOLDER CONCERNS

Key Issues

Key players	Celebrating	Instructing	Marketing Blaine	Minimizing costs	Safety
Traditionalists	✓✓✓✓✓	✓	✓	✓	✓
Modernists	✓✓	✓✓✓✓✓			
Local merchants (and similar groups)	✓✓✓✓✓	✓	✓✓✓✓	✓✓✓	✓
Residents/taxpayers (not directly involved)	✓✓✓	✓✓✓	✓✓✓	✓✓✓✓	✓✓✓✓
Elected officials	✓✓✓✓	✓✓	✓✓✓✓✓	✓✓✓	✓✓✓
Educators	✓	✓✓✓✓✓	✓	✓✓✓	✓
Public safety officials	✓	✓	✓	✓	✓✓✓✓✓

Bill reads Connie's assessment and scans her grid with interest. Then he puts them back down on the table. Although he is smiling slightly, he also has a pained look around his eyes, as if he has a headache coming on.

BILL: Interesting stuff, Connie. But my takeaway from all this is that what we have here is a goddamn mess, with nobody agreeing on anything. Modernists and traditionalists, for pete's sake!

CONNIE: [*laughs*] OK, maybe it looks like a big mess when it's boiled down to shorthand and little check marks on a grid, Bill. But actually, my sense is that you've got quite a lot to work with here. People disagree on lots of things, but a lot of people out there want this thing to succeed. All you have to do is find a way to bring these people and groups together and *harness* that energy, while you keep your eye on the groups that have specific objections. I think I can help you with that, if you're willing to keep playing by a different set of rules than I think you're accustomed to.

BILL: I'll be honest with you. June isn't that far away. It looks to me like the way you propose to work, it may take *another* two hundred years to plan this party. But Mike seems to have a lot of confidence in you. And to be honest, I didn't get very far doing it my way. So I'm willing to move forward with you taking the lead on the process. But I reserve the right to blow the whistle if I think you're getting off track.

CONNIE: Fair enough.

Go, or no go?

This brings us to the last step in the convening phase: the decision to move ahead with consensus building or *not* to move ahead. That decision grows out of the convener's ability to say yes to the following four questions:

- Can we get the right people to participate?
- Do we have adequate resources for this project?
- Is there sufficient time?
- Do we have agreement on preliminary ground rules?

In this example, Bill and Connie are most of the way there. First, and most important, the key people—starting with Bill—seem to be open to consensus building. (Bill, of course, still needs to see results.) Connie is confident that she has identified the key stakeholder groups and that she can get qualified and committed people (a first-choice person and an alternate) to represent each group. While there are clearly issues about paying for the celebration itself, she has no concerns about resources for the consensus-building process.

The timing issue looms large: with an inflexible June deadline, only a few months away, the Blaine Bicentennial Committee will have to achieve consensus sooner, rather than later. (Connie's previous experience with consensus building, at the local community college, did not face this kind of schedule pressure.) And finally, based on what she's heard from Bill and the other stakeholders, Connie still has to come up with a project work plan, a set of proposed ground rules, and get the interested parties to agree to some version of both.

Our next chapter focuses on the realities of what we call "facilitative leadership." In order for a group like this to reach an agreement, somebody has to play a facilitative or mediating role. There are other important roles that need to be played, as well. The consensus-building group's first shared task, therefore, is to assign roles and responsibilities.

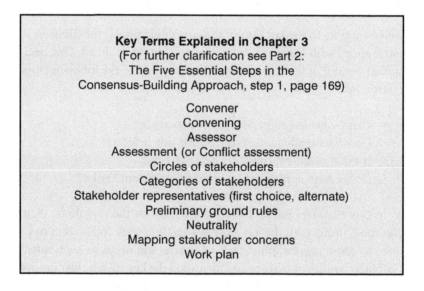

Key Terms Explained in Chapter 3
(For further clarification see Part 2:
The Five Essential Steps in the
Consensus-Building Approach, step 1, page 169)

Convener
Convening
Assessor
Assessment (or Conflict assessment)
Circles of stakeholders
Categories of stakeholders
Stakeholder representatives (first choice, alternate)
Preliminary ground rules
Neutrality
Mapping stakeholder concerns
Work plan

4

~

Assigning Tasks and Leadership Responsibilities

In previous chapters, we've described the group dynamics dictated by Robert's Rules—a parliamentary approach that, at the end of the day, is all about **process**.

But another way to compare Robert's Rules with CBA is to look at the **players** involved. What roles do they play? What are their respective responsibilities? Perhaps most important, where does leadership come from, and how is it exercised?

In parliamentary procedure, there are really only four players. These are: the **public at large**, the **deliberative body** (which we'll consider collectively as one player), the **moderator** (or chair), and in some cases, the **parliamentarian**.

Let's look briefly at their roles and responsibilities. The general public is at least one step removed from the action. It is almost entirely reactive, responding or failing to respond to the actions of a deliberative body like a town meeting. If the public gets angry enough about one or more issues, they can change the composition of the deliberative body, for example, at the ballot box. The deliberative body proposes and disposes, following the tight script laid down by Robert's Rules. The moderator enforces that script, much like a director runs a film crew:

handing out assignments, setting the pace, deciding when it's time to move on. The parliamentarian (who is sometimes the same person as the moderator, but not always) serves as the in-house rules expert, weighing in like a referee at a football game: *this* action is within the rules, but *that* action is not.

Most of these roles are passive. Voters go to the polls only infrequently (and many don't go at all). The members of the deliberative body are supposed to do their homework, but many don't. Yes, some members of that body draw up articles or motions, and then get up to present and defend them, while others may rise to oppose them. Experts may be called upon for testimony by either side. However, the vast majority of the members of a deliberative body wind up simply listening and reacting to what happens. Their options, moreover, are severely restricted by Robert's Rules.

The parliamentarian mainly speaks when spoken to. He generally only "blows the whistle" when asked for an opinion about a procedural point. Think of the first-base or third-base umpire, when the catcher appeals the home-plate umpire's call that the batter has checked his swing. If *asked*, the third-base umpire may (or may not) call a strike on that left-handed batter. Similarly, it's rare for the parliamentarian to actively inject himself or herself into the debate.

That leaves the moderator, who is by far the most active player. Depending on his or her style, the moderator really does set the pace, the tone, and to some extent even the agenda of the meeting. Although a parliamentary process may involve dozens or even hundreds of players, only a handful of players actually initiate anything, or contribute ideas or solutions. In a very real sense, the active and passive players alike have relatively few options. They can't take responsibility even if they want to. They are ruled by Robert's Rules.

Getting more players into the game

In CBA, many more people are called upon to take an active problem-solving role—doing work that engages them in what's happening, learning about the problem, and working to craft a solution. They do so in ways that are extremely flexible. Tasks (and the groups charged with performing them) often overlap. The same individual may play different roles at different points in the consensus-building process. The overall goal is to get the best ideas on the table and combine them in the most creative ways possible. The process adjusts to meet this overall goal.

Involving more people increases the chances that good ideas will see the light of day and be dealt with in ways that build consensus. It also spreads the workload across a broader base. This is important, because engaging in active and effective problem solving generally requires more effort than simply following Robert's Rules.

Who are these players? The following is a sample list; you may omit some of these players or categories in some situations, or include others:

- The **convener**
- The **assessor**
- **Stakeholders (or constituents)**
- The **consensus building group (stakeholder representatives)**
- The **executive committee (or steering committee)**
- The **chair**
- The **process manager (or facilitator)**
- The **recorder**
- **Subcommittees (or subgroups)**
- **Expert advisors**

Let's look at each of these roles, focusing on the responsibilities that each is expected to assume in the consensus-building process. We will present them roughly in the order they might appear in a typical consensus-building effort.

The convener and the assessor

We've already described the role of the convener at length in chapter 3, so we'll only summarize that role here. The convener initiates the dialogue, assesses the chances of achieving resolution (sometimes on her own, or sometimes by tapping a skilled assessor), identifies the essential participants, and handles several other important chores before scheduling the first organizational meeting.

Stakeholders or constituents

Logically, you could make the case that the stakeholders, or constituents, should appear first on our list, since at least some of them are probably already on the scene long before the convener shows up. On the other hand, as explained in chapter 3, the convener and the assessor play important roles in identifying constituent groups, sometimes including those (like future generations) who aren't yet able to speak for themselves.

It's possible to imagine a dispute in which each stakeholder group (or category of stakeholders) consists of a single stakeholder, and there is a very small number of interested parties. In such a case, there might be a complete, one-to-one overlap between the stakeholders and the consensus-building group. There would be no need for a separate executive committee, as described below. Most significant public disputes, though, don't fit this profile. Most of the time they involve large numbers of groups, each of which contains more than a few people. Some groups may need more than one representative at the table (although this raises the issue of "balance" with other groups). For example: there may only be five interested groups, but each may require four people to represent the spectrum of interests within it, resulting in a total of twenty people at the table.

Typically, all stakeholders and constituent groups are encouraged to observe the consensus-building proceedings and learn as much as they can about the effort. As a rule, they are *not* encouraged to voice their opinions in response to developments at the table. Instead, they are encouraged to communicate their views through their official or unofficial representative(s).

A word about "representation": when we use the word "represent," we don't necessarily mean "elected by." When someone says, "I represent Group X," they're generally better off having some sort of vote behind them, validating that statement. (This is something that the convener will certainly keep track of.) But there's another valid kind of representation, which we summarize as *speaking in the style of*. This may sound a little strange, but it's actually quite common. To cite a private-sector example, when a multifunctional task force is called together, the heads of those functional areas tend to pick someone who has a good "feel" for his own area. There may be a lot of people above "old Joe" in the manufacturing hierarchy, but everyone knows that Joe has his finger on the pulse of manufacturing and expresses that point of view extremely well. He *speaks in the style of* his manufacturing colleagues. They are likely to be comfortable knowing he's in there pitching for them.

A good convener knows how to find the equivalent of Joe and also how to blend elected representatives and speak-in-the-style-of representatives.

The consensus-building group

This is the group that actually sits down at the table to do the heavy lifting. It consists of the representatives whom the convener has invited to the table, or in some cases, the representatives whom a particular constituency has chosen with the encouragement and help of the convener.

Everyone else in the process revolves around this group, and all of their efforts are aimed at helping this group succeed. Once assembled by the convener, this group effectively calls the shots: approving ground rules, schedules, and budgets, which in many cases involves keying off of a work plan that has already been drafted by the assessor. Nevertheless, the convener can't anticipate everything that will happen when this group assembles for the first time. Unexpected things will occur, and new rules will be needed, as the group gets down to work.

Note our emphasis on the centrality of this group. Advocates of Robert's Rules would no doubt say the same sort of thing: their process puts the deliberative body at the heart of the action. True enough, but it also *subordinates* those people to that process. In CBA, the group stays on top of the process.

The executive committee

"Executive committee" may be too formal a term, since it conjures up images of private-sector types in walnut-paneled boardrooms. A good alternative would be "steering committee," since what we're talking about is a smaller group that helps steer a larger group, rather than a group that makes those so-called executive-level decisions.

Some consensus-building groups need an executive committee; others don't. Generally, the larger the group, the more likely it is that it will need some subset of people who can get together and "steer" the process. If so, it should be composed of a few individuals selected by the full group, each of whom represents a crucial constituency whose interests must be addressed if the problem at hand is going to be resolved.

The chair

Sometimes when people hear the phrase *consensus building*, they hear something else as well: *nobody in charge*. Nothing could be farther from the truth. There are lots of leaders in consensus building, including what we call the "chair." We use this term to refer to the person who formally presides at each meeting, ensures that the parties work together in a businesslike way, and in some cases serves as the group's external spokesperson.

Sometimes, the chair is the person who got the whole process started in the first place—the one who called in the convener and loaned that individual enough credibility to get the job done. In other cases, the chair and the convener are the same person. (In both of these situations, of course, it helps enormously if the individual who becomes chair commands widespread respect and isn't seen as partisan.) In still other cases, there is no chair until the consensus-building group organizes itself to select one.

Ultimately, the process demands a chair (who is also a member of the executive committee, if there is one). Once again, we stress that the chair *does not* come up with the answers. Except for certain at-the-table procedures, the chair doesn't manage the process—that's the task of our next player. Instead, the chair is the voice and the conscience of the process, both at the table and away from the table. The chair has to pick her words carefully, not only to keep options open but also to build support for the process. These are unusual and important skills, which if well exercised can make consensus building far easier.

The process manager (or facilitator)

Somewhere early in the process, the consensus-building group must identify the individual who is going to *manage* the dialogue. This is a distinctly different role from that of the chair.

Sometimes called a "facilitator" or "mediator," the process manager's main responsibility is to keep participants focused and make sure that the consensus-building process doesn't get off track. Since we'll describe the process manager at work the next few chapters, we won't provide a lengthy description here.

For the purposes of this overview, moreover, we won't dig down into the differences between facilitators and mediators. (Briefly stated, facilitators deal with people face-to-face around the table. Mediators do that and also deal with the parties *away* from the table, shuttling among various stakeholder groups between meetings.) For the sake of convenience, however, we will use the terms interchangeably.

Who can serve as a facilitator? The answer really depends on the scope and intensity of the debate. If the situation involves a number of parties who are already in serious conflict, and if it looks like more than a few meetings are going to be needed to solve the problem, the consensus-building group should think seriously about hiring a professional facilitator to guide their efforts. Facilitators are hired just like any other consultants—that is, based on interviews, references, fee schedules, and so on—although always with an eye toward making sure that no group feels "railroaded" in the choice.

In a less drawn-out debate, it's possible for the convener or the chair to continue on as facilitator. In the private sector, this happens all the time: someone has a task to accomplish that cuts across divisions or functions, and he calls a group together, states the problem, and manages the discussion through to a shared conclusion.

In either case, the group must clearly define *in writing* the facilitator's responsibilities and then pick a person acceptable to all members of the group. (In the case of larger efforts, the executive committee may handle both of these tasks.) Writing the job description in some detail is particularly important, so that there is no subsequent confusion.

Here is a sample job description:

WANTED: Professional facilitator or facilitation team to assist consensus-building group. Tasks include: preparation of meeting agendas and background materials, note-taking during meetings, coordination of subcommittee input, preparation of meeting summaries, and overall management of all group deliberations. Must have relevant training and experience. Good sense of humor a plus!

The recorder

The group also needs to decide who will serve as its recorder, in other words, the scribe who will produce written summaries every time the stakeholder representatives get together.

Depending on the ground rules agreed to by the group, the recording task may consist of several distinct functions. Most groups find it helpful to keep the discussion focused by having ideas written down on a flip chart in real time as those ideas are generated by the members of the group. Most likely, you've been in a situation where someone is scribbling highlights on big pads and then sticking them up on the walls. That's what we're talking about.

Maybe you've also been in a situation where the recorder was an accomplished cartoonist or artist—an individual who used multicolored markers, cute illustrations, and lots of swooping arrows and three-dimensional exclamation points to "capture" the discussion. In our experience, these recorders, although talented, can be highly distracting. Members of the group start watching out of the corner of their eyes to see how they and their ideas are being depicted. The artist *may* appear to be editorializing, rather than simply reporting.

When the recorder starts dominating the discussion, something is amiss. The goal, pure and simple, is to put the key concepts up on the wall in the sparest possible language, so that the discussion can move forward, building on ideas that have already been suggested. People are less inclined to repeat themselves, or restate the opinions of others, if what's been said is already up on the wall in big letters. This point is made the first time the recorder listens to a heartfelt reiteration, then goes back and underlines the previous version of that comment.

Nor should logistics be allowed to intrude. In the case of a large group, it may be useful to go to electronic projection of computer-generated notes, so that all the members of the group can see the emerging product easily. A general rule of thumb is that *the best recorder is the one you don't notice.*

Who can serve as a recorder? Sometimes the recorder is a paid member of the professional facilitator's team. Sometimes he or she is a volunteer from the executive committee. The key skill, in all cases, is the ability to *follow a conversation* and translate what is being said into simple words or phrases. (Legible handwriting is part of the job description, too.)

The recorder, it should be noted, does not act alone. Group members should periodically review the ideas that have been recorded to confirm that the work accurately reflects the views of the members.

In addition to real-time documentation, the recorder also assumes responsibility for writing up brief summaries after each meeting. These summaries usually include only major points of agreement and disagreement, without attributing specific positions to individuals. (The first such summary is always the hardest, as people learn to leave behind their preconceptions about "minutes.")

In small groups with volunteer recorders, the group should keep an eye on two issues: whether the recorder is suffering from burn-out, and whether the recorder's assignment needs to be rotated for political or other reasons. In other words, if the recording function starts to be an issue, *change* something.

Subcommittees

Subcommittees (or subgroups, task forces, or whatever your group chooses to call them) can serve several roles. Most importantly, they can serve as idea-generators or fact-finders: the source of new proposals, possible solutions, or careful summaries of conflicting data. This is particularly important in very large consensus-building efforts, in which a collection of stakeholder groups may decide to send several representatives into subgroups to review topics of special concern to them. The products of these discussions may be blended and refined by the facilitator, or by the executive committee, for presentation to the full group.

A second role for subcommittees, again most often seen in the context of large groups, falls under the umbrella of housekeeping. It makes no sense, for example, for every member of a large consensus-building effort to be responsible for looking after the group's budget. For efficiency's sake, the group may choose to establish a budget subcommittee, most likely including a member from each of the key stakeholder categories. Or it may choose to invest these responsibilities in the executive/steering committee.

Expert advisors

We have left to last a group of people who, in an indirect way, throw into sharp relief the key differences between Robert's Rules and consensus building. In the world of Robert's Rules, these people are called "expert witnesses." In CBA, they are called "expert advisors."

Expert witnesses are often called upon to testify for or against proposed legislation or regulations, based on what they perceive to be its technical strengths or flaws. Yet, no sooner do they leave the table than another expert witness—hired by the other side—sits down and says (or appears to say) the exact opposite of what's just been said. This is sometimes summed up in the phrase "dueling scientists." It leads laypeople to throw up their hands and say, "Well, since we can't figure out the technical merits of this issue, let's look for some other way to decide." When the issue has technical considerations at its heart, however, this can lead to disaster.

Expert advisors, by contrast, bring to the table specialized knowledge to which the entire group has equal access. The point is to establish a baseline of shared information, and to move on from there. In CBA, the group works to get beyond fighting over baseline facts, even if they interpret those facts differently. It first agrees on a set of questions, choose advisors together, listens to the information offered by those advisors, and then generates solutions that embrace both the facts and the interests of the stakeholders.

Back to Blaine

When we last heard from our somewhat imaginary town of Blaine, Bill had agreed to let Connie take their budding consensus-building effort to the next step. This involved bringing the four key players, whom Connie had already identified, to the table. (Bill, of course, was a fifth key player.) With Connie's encouragement, Bill sent a copy of Connie's six-paragraph assessment to each of these players. (She and Bill decided *not* to share her grid, at this point, worrying that it might focus people on their disagreements rather than on points of agreement.) In his accompanying letter, Bill stressed that Connie's assessment, which they had all seen in an earlier form, was only a draft and that he hoped it would serve as an effective jumping-off point for more discussion. He invited these four individuals to a meeting in the basement conference room at city hall the following Tuesday evening.

To his surprise, all four called his office on the day they received his letter and accepted. Two of them even congratulated him on a job well done.

We have already met these individuals in chapter 3. (Remember that we're giving them names that resonate with their individual roles and styles—like Bill who likes to be "boss" and Connie who sees herself as a consensus builder.) They are:

- **Vince.** Vince believes in *voting*. He sees 51 percent as the American Way—a good way to end an endless debate and set limits on a strong leader.
- **Sally.** Sally wants to keep it *simple*. As soon as a process starts to get too complicated for her taste, Sally forcefully reminds people of what she considers to be the Golden Rule of politics: KISS (keep it simple, stupid).
- **Ralph.** Ralph is in favor of more *research*. He constantly reminds those around him that nothing is as simple as it seems. If you rush to judgment, he cautions, you're likely to rush to the wrong judgment.
- **Molly.** Molly is a *moralist*. She believes that no important decisions should be made in a moral vacuum and that all the facts in the world don't necessarily add up to a morally defensible conclusion.

The diagram on the next page, called the *Cast of Characters in Blaine*, may be a useful reminder of who's who.

On Tuesday evening at 7:00 p.m.—the scheduled meeting time—everyone was seated around the oversized conference table under the buzzing fluorescent lights. Bill admitted to himself that he was pleasantly surprised that these volunteers had all appeared on time, ready to do business. He called the meeting to order:

BILL: Since we're all here, we should probably get started. Thanks for coming tonight, and agreeing to help out with this process. Maybe we should begin by introducing ourselves. I'll go first. I run Blaine Manufacturing, which I think you've all heard of. As Connie's write-up explained, Mike, our mayor, asked me to help out with this bicentennial thing. He also loaned Connie to me on a part-time basis. And as you've already seen, Connie has some interesting ideas about how we might move forward.

Connie, do you want to pick up the story there?

CAST OF CHARACTERS IN BLAINE

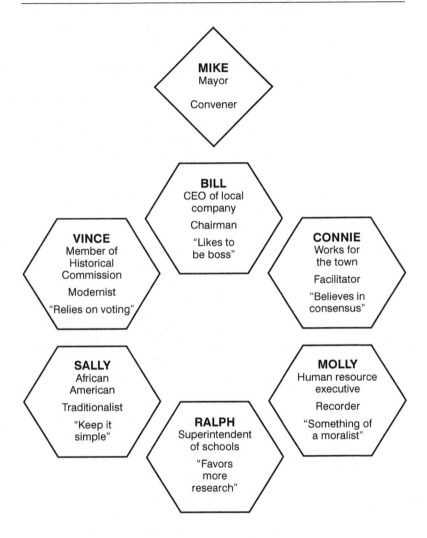

CONNIE: Sure. First, me: I used to work at the community college, and now I'm with the Youth Department, where I run programs and serve as the liaison with the school and parks departments.

> While I was at the college, I did some work trying to help solve a difficult internal governance problem. In that context, I became familiar with this process called "the consensus building approach" or CBA for short. I think that's one reason why Mike offered me my current job—he said he liked the idea of having somebody around who likes to solve problems. So when Bill invited me to get involved, and Mike said yes, I was happy to jump in. Since that time, I've talked with a lot of people—including all of you—and written up the draft summary that Bill sent to each of you.

> Maybe we could keep going around the table in this direction, and as you introduce yourself, you could say something about how you'd like to see this bicentennial celebration handled.

VINCE: Well, I guess that means that I go next. I'm Vince, and as a couple of you already know, I'm a physician who runs a practice and still makes the occasional house call, believe it or not. As such, I'm out flat a lot of the time. If my cell doesn't go off during this meeting, I'll be pleasantly surprised.

> I think it's important to make time for community activities, including the Historical Commission, which I've served on for twelve years, mainly because I'm a history buff and my family's been in this area for a couple of generations.

> And to answer your question, Connie, I'm frankly a little suspicious of this whole bicentennial effort. As I told Bill the first time we talked about this on the phone, I don't want to be involved in any kind of whitewash of our history. So I was happy to read the thing that Connie wrote, which raised this whole issue of traditionalists and mod-

ernists. I guess I'm a modernist, although for sure, no one's ever called me *that* before!

I guess I should add that I'm also a little wary about this so-called consensus-building process. I'm inclined to think that we put people in office and pay them money to deal with things like this. As a rule, I subscribe to the idea that you put the issue on the table, and put it to a vote.

CONNIE: Perfect—a very clear picture of where you're coming from. Sally?

SALLY: Well, I suppose it's an accident, but you've got a traditionalist sitting next to a modernist. I'm Sally, and my husband is the minister at the First Baptist Church, which is the largest primarily minority congregation in this part of the state. I run the Clergy Support Association, which as you may know is a volunteer group that tries to help all of the religious leaders in the town, and recently, the county. So I get around a lot.

Being black, I also deal with stereotypes a lot. Maybe you guys thought a black woman would come in here thumping the tub, arguing that this celebration has to deal with past injustices, and so on. Well, I don't see it that way. I think we have to move forward *as a community*, not as a collection of groups with old grievances.

As for this process, I don't know much about it, so I'll keep an open mind. In general, though, I see a lot of people who—for whatever reason—stop things from happening by making them too complicated. In my work around town, I'm always telling people to "keep it simple." With all due respect, Connie, I wonder if you're making things too complicated.

CONNIE: [*laughs*] Well, folks, I get the sense that being shy isn't going to be a problem at this table. Thanks for saying it as you see it, Sally. Who's next?

RALPH: I guess I am. I'm Ralph, and I'm your superintendent of schools. I've run into a lot of you in that role. Bill's company has been extremely supportive of the school system over the years. And Connie has done a terrific job in bringing the town departments that deal directly with kids into a good working relationship.

I guess I should have been seated somewhere between Vince and Sally. I tend to agree with Vince that this bicentennial celebration is an important opportunity to tell the real story of Blaine, which, by the way, is nothing to be ashamed of. If we're going to invoke history, I think it has to be a true history.

As for process . . . well, Sally, I guess I'm one of those people you were talking about, who like to make things complicated. I honestly think that if you don't get at the complexity of an issue, you can't possibly get to the right answers. I'd rather go slowly and get it right.

SALLY: So your implication is that people like me tend to get it wrong?

CONNIE: Whoa. Bill, it might be time to invoke ground rule #1.

BILL: Uh, sure. Connie and I established one ground rule in advance of this meeting, which the chair of the meeting—that's me—is supposed to enforce. We have to agree to disagree without being disagreeable. And those of you who know me, including Sally, know that I'm going to have the hardest time of *anybody* with that particular rule. But let's agree to that rule, for now. And we can agree to other rules if the group decides to go that way.

CONNIE: Well stated, Bill. Who's next? Molly?

MOLLY: Saving the best for last. I'm Molly. I'm the head of human resources at Informed Systems, which is Blaine's claim to fame in the Information Age. At work, I try to keep the twenty-somethings and the forty-somethings working cooperatively.

I'm also heavily involved in services to Blaine's senior citizens. I've been the head of Meals on Wheels, and more recently I've chaired Blaine Residences for the Elderly, the nonprofit that manages our three subsidized housing complexes for senior citizens.

I don't know where I come down on this traditional versus modernist thing, mainly because I haven't thought about it much. But I tend to look at the world in terms of just doing what's right, which usually strikes me as kind of obvious. I mean, you get in there, you figure it out, and you do the right thing.

I guess I don't have any strong feelings about this process that you two seem to be proposing. Except that I'd hate to see some sort of big, brokered compromise that was everybody's second-favorite solution.

CONNIE: Well, that's something we will try hard to avoid. Thanks, Molly.

Bill, I think we have to cycle back to you one more time, since I asked my question after you introduced yourself. How do *you* think this bicentennial celebration should be handled?

BILL: Not gonna let me off the hook, eh, Connie? OK. And I should start by saying that in business, I generally chair the meetings, and everybody looks to me for the final decision. Connie has already warned me that chairing this process is going to be different.

To be candid, I have my doubts about this process, at least as I understand it so far. We only have a couple of months to deliver something, and the mayor has made it clear that he's counting on us. Still in the spirit of candor, I called Vince a few weeks back, and at the end of that conversation, I would have bet that there was no chance that he would wind up wanting to help out. Zero chance. And that would have been a loss, because—like the rest of you—Vince is somebody who holds a lot of sway in this town. In addition to being our resident historian, of course.

Having said that, I have to say I'm a lot closer to where Sally is, in terms of what we actually ought to put out there in front of the town. I can't see bringing a lot of skeletons out of the closet and throwing a parade for them.

SALLY: Hear, hear. Let those skeletons lie.

CONNIE: OK, I think we've accomplished what I hoped to get done with that exercise, which is to figure out what each of us brings to the table. I don't want you guys digging in and arguing for one position or another at this point.

Instead, what I'd like to do is spend some time going over the preliminary work plan that I've drawn up, which focuses on things like schedule, milestones, budget, and so on. I also want to get some agreement on who's going to do what, as we launch into this consensus-building process. And finally, I'd also like to talk about ground rules. Bill and I have proposed the one that we've already told you about, and which we hope you'll want to stick with, but there are some others that we have to agree on.

Over the next hour, the group reviewed Connie's work plan, which they agreed was ambitious but doable. They then agreed that Bill—to whom the mayor had assigned the task of leading the effort—should continue to chair the meetings. When Connie explained the recorder's role, Molly volunteered to take that job. (The group reserved the right to rotate the position at some later point, if that seemed appropriate.) Connie explained the facilitator's role, and the group unanimously agreed that she should make the transition from assessor to facilitator. Bill and Ralph offered to serve as a budget subcommittee, to which everyone agreed, but only after Vince sought and got the assurance that no expenditures would be made without the consent of the larger committee.

As for ground rules, the group agreed to the following:

- Bill, as chair, would be the only person authorized to speak to the press on behalf of the group. Anyone else could speak to whomever they wanted about their own views, but they would *not* represent the opinions of other people at the table.
- At the urging of Ralph, the group agreed to consider itself a public body, and to post all of its meetings in conformance with the state's Open Meeting law. Bill expressed some reluctance, worrying that this increased the chances of "things turning into a circus," but Ralph said that in his position as superintendent he couldn't afford to risk running afoul of the law, which was sometimes difficult to interpret. Anyway, he pointed out, in most cases the surest way to get the press *not* to come to a meeting was to post it. Observers (from the press or otherwise) would be welcome, but they would not be permitted to speak at the table.
- The group agreed that all of its meetings would take place face-to-face, rather than online or by means of teleconferencing. "I like to look people in the eye," Vince explained. The group agreed.
- Everyone agreed that Connie should prepare a short summary of what was accomplished at each meeting. After everyone had a chance to review it in depth, it would become part of the permanent record.

The group agreed to meet again the following Tuesday evening. Connie asked the group if she could invite the Historical Commission (of which Vince was a member) to make a fifteen-minute presentation at that next meeting, focusing on potential key themes for the celebration.

"As long as they keep the word 'celebration' in mind," Sally said.

"Oh, we will," Vince responded in a neutral tone. "And we'll also keep history in mind."

Ralph said he would also get copies of the high school's Blaine history module into the hands of all committee members before the end of the week, so that they would have yet another frame of reference. "It's a good module, used in our AP history course," he said, "and we've put a lot of time into it." Bill wondered aloud if the town's public safety departments should be asked to talk about parades and celebrations in general, and the group agreed to add the police chief to the next week's agenda.

Reflections on leadership

One of the subtexts in the dialogue just presented has to do with *leadership*. In his private sector context, Bill is accustomed to hearing people out, and then telling people his decision. And because he controls the purse strings, Bill's word is law and implementation of his decisions is more or less automatic.

Vince's comment ("we put people in office and pay them money to deal with things like this") reflects the public sector equivalent. Isn't "leadership" about making the tough decision? "The buck stops here," read the little sign on Harry Truman's desk, and—in theory, at least— people *liked* the image of a tough little guy making difficult decisions, saying the equivalent of "damn the torpedoes; full speed ahead!"

People forget, though, that Truman was massively unpopular in his own time and barely won reelection. The truth is, when it comes to top-down leadership, we only want the buck to stop on the desk of someone who *agrees* with us and makes tough decisions with which we agree. If he or she goes the other way, we call them "dictatorial" or "tyrannical," and begin trying to unseat or undermine them.

Conversely, top-down leadership strips us of our motivation to participate. It fuels the downward spiral of disillusionment and disengagement that characterizes many of today's public debates. "Don't vote," reads the cynical bumper-sticker, "it only encourages them."

Leadership in a CBA context is different. It's about having the ability to bring people to an informed understanding of what their choices are, helping them evaluate the merits of each possible option, and encouraging them to search for a package that will be mutually advanta-

*PART

outcomes

geous. In chapter 2, we introduced the concept of "facilitative leadership," which we contrasted with images of the leader as savior or shepherd. Facilitative leadership is not about "yoking and yanking," or about getting people to go where you have already decided they need to wind up. Instead, the successful leader encourages a rigorous thinking-through—that is, a systematic and self-conscious process of reflection—on the part of those who will be most affected by a decision.

Facilitative leadership is not the same thing as "being nice," or even "being fair." Instead, it's all about keeping one's eye on the prize, and that means getting to an agreement that is seen by all parties as fair, efficient, and wise. If it is seen as having these attributes, it will also be *durable*, which is the final characteristic of a good solution. (A fair, wise, and efficient solution will *stick*.)

Getting to this kind of solution is almost never easy. It requires bringing people in to a new and sometimes uncomfortable process, making them feel valued—not by tricking them but by valuing them—and getting them to try on new ideas for size. It involves sharing power as broadly as possible, which to most leaders feels, well, *odd*. (Wasn't I elected? Aren't I better at this than most people?) Sharing power is a critical part of getting people to take responsibility for their own futures. In a very real way, it gets back to the origins of democracy, which assumed that *all* citizens had an important role to play.

In chapter 5, we get into the nuts and bolts of problem solving, in which good ideas are raised, debated, and refined, most likely in combination with other good ideas. We also listen in as the Blaine Bicentennial Committee starts getting its arms around its assignment and around the process of consensus building.

Key Terms Explained in Chapter 4
(For further clarification see Part 2:
The Five Essential Steps in the
Consensus Building Approach, step 2, page 173)

Robert's Rules of Order
Deliberative body
Moderator
Parliamentarian
CBA
Constituents (stakeholders)
Consensus-building group (stakeholder representatives)
Elected representatives
Speak-in-the-style of representatives
Chair
Facilitator
Executive committee (steering committee)
Recorder
Subcommittees
Expert advisors
Meeting summaries

5

~

The Importance of Facilitation

As we've described in previous chapters, CBA requires careful preparation. That means identifying the right people, assessing the problem
accurately, thinking through a work plan and budget, setting up at least
a preliminary set of ground rules so that people can start to work together at the table, and then getting the right people to join the effort.
Once they're at the table, roles and responsibilities must be assigned.

But this is all "table-setting," in a sense, for the problem-solving
process that is to follow. How do people start talking in a way that
builds consensus on a solution, or an agreement?

Every consensus-building process is different. Working backward
from a number of very successful deliberations, in a broad range of
contexts, we can identify eight features of successful consensus-building
deliberations. Those eight features (illustrated by a couple of visits to
our friends in Blaine) constitute the heart of this chapter. First, let's
look at the tone that should dominate your deliberations—and the
mind-set that gives rise to that tone.

Building the problem-solving mind-set

Simply put, the people at the table need to get into a problem-solving mind-set as soon as possible. It's unrealistic to assume that everyone will arrive at the table in that frame of mind. More likely, people will become "believers" over time, as they see the consensus-building process making real progress. Assuming that people come to the table in a confrontational, winner-take-all frame of mind—the Robert's Rules frame of mind—the convener's and facilitator's goal must be to keep people's minds open to learning a new way of doing things.

One way to achieve this is to **be explicit up front about the ultimate goal of the effort**. Some of this should have already gone on during the convening step. Now it needs to happen in the group setting, at the table. Simply put, the goal is to reach consensus. This needs to be explained, emphasized, and reinforced. Consensus doesn't mean, "I win; you lose." It means, **we all come out ahead**. It doesn't mean that we trade horses and logroll our way to a bare majority, and ignore the angry, losing minorities that are created. It means that we collectively find a solution that's satisfactory to everyone (or almost everyone).

A second technique for building the problem-solving mind-set is to **be explicit up front about the process itself**. Oftentimes, people need reassurance that there is a structure to the dialogue. That structure is detailed in this chapter and later chapters. In broad-brush terms, the facilitator should tell the group what to expect along the way.

A third key technique for helping people get into a problem-solving mind-set is to **elicit a nonconfrontational statement of initial concerns**. In chapter 4, we saw how Connie accomplished this. The question she put to the group, in so many words, was this: Based on the assessment you've read and the individual conversations we've had, what's your personal starting point? Where do you come down on the bicentennial celebration, and what's your take on this proposed consensus-building process?

To some extent, Connie was lucky. Nobody took that opportunity to try to blow anyone else out of the water. Everyone at the table, even the skeptics, gave their views (on the bicentennial) without being too confrontational, although there was a testy moment or two. Everyone seemed willing to give the process a try, although one or two people grumbled about inefficiency or wondered aloud why their elected officials didn't just take care of the problem.

Connie also did two things that helped build the problem-solving mind-set. First, she **made sure everyone was heard**, and got roughly equal airtime. There's nothing worse than to have one or more groups conclude at the outset that the proceedings are going to be dominated by somebody else and that their interests won't be served. Such "oppressed minorities" can undermine the whole process later on; so the goal, at the outset, is to keep this from happening.

Second, Connie **set limits on the opening statements**. This may sound a little strange: didn't we just imply that CBA is all about being heard? The answer is yes, but it is also about inventing new proposals. We've already mentioned the tendency of certain kinds of people—elected officials, for example—to embrace a position publicly and then stick to it, even after that position stops making much sense. Therefore, the goal at the outset is to get opening statements out on the table but not to have individuals or groups talk in absolutist, uncompromising terms.

You want the people at your table to say, "This is what's important to me." You don't want them to go on to say, "And I don't care what's important to the rest of you jerks, and I never will!"

We're talking about heading off this kind of "absolutism" before it takes root. Keep in mind that in the early stages, absolutism can show up in strange places. If someone has come to the table itching for a fight, then something as simple as setting the next meeting date may send that itchy person around the bend. The facilitator has to head this off. (Note the important role played by the facilitator, from the very earliest step in the process.) In the following pages, we'll present more ideas for heading off and defusing seemingly "non-negotiable" opening demands.

Again: our emphasis is on **building trust**, and **fostering the right frame of mind to move forward as a group**. As you read about the eight features of successful deliberations in the following pages, think about the opportunities that each presents for building a problem-solving mind-set.

Eight steps toward consensus

Every consensus-building process follows its own particular course. Nevertheless, there are eight features of almost all successful CBA-style deliberations. We'll present them as an action agenda in roughly the order they are likely to present themselves. They are:

1. Pursue deliberations in a nonjudgmental fashion.
2. Separate "inventing" from "committing."
3. Create subcommittees and seek expert input when appropriate.
4. Use a single-text procedure.
5. Modify the agenda and ground rules as necessary.
6. Set a hard deadline for ending deliberations.
7. Build on prior relationships.
8. Emphasize mutual gain.

Pursue deliberations in a nonjudgmental fashion

People have to agree to work together in constructive ways. When Connie and Bill set the preliminary ground rules for the group's first meeting, they decided to establish only one such rule: to agree to disagree without being disagreeable. Consensus building isn't about being "nice." On the other hand, it's also about not attacking the motives or character of others. The point is to disagree on issues of substance, in ways that are not intentionally offensive to others.

On a related point, people have to concentrate on **hearing** and **being heard**. Most people don't practice the art of listening; therefore, they're not very good at hearing other people. One way to become a better listener is to **attempt to restate the other person's position,**

accurately and succinctly. If you can do that to the other person's satisfaction, you're listening well.

At the same time, you have to be heard yourself. If you don't speak up, you can't advocate your own interests, let alone those of the group that you are supposed to be representing. If someone attempts to summarize or "play back" what you've said, make sure they get it right. This not only avoids the "oppressed minority" problem described above, it also increases the chances that your interests will be fully reflected in the final agreement. In deliberations governed by Robert's Rules, people sometimes serve their interests best by concealing their motives. Not so in CBA, which calls for "transparency." The more transparent you are, the better—and you can't be penalized for your candor.

In the same spirit, people participate constructively in consensus building by **giving reasons**. What does this mean? Participants have to learn to distinguish between their **positions** and their **interests**. (CBA is about serving people's interests.) When somebody states a strongly held requirement (a position), they're actually presenting what they see as the only, or the best, solution to the problem. What the group needs to hear are the reasons behind that belief (interests). They need to hear a clear statement of the individual's perception of the problem, and their reasoning regarding the "best" solution. There are two compelling arguments for this: (1) it forces each individual to figure out exactly what is and isn't important to them, and (2) it enables the group to understand each individual's interests, and why they are perceived as important, opening the door to other mutually advantageous solutions.

Let's imagine that at the end of that first meeting in Blaine, described toward the end of chapter 4, Connie decides to raise the issue of exactly when the town should celebrate its bicentennial. (In real life, assuming that Connie is a reasonably skilled facilitator, this issue probably wouldn't come up quite so soon.) But, let's assume it does, and Connie puts some possibilities before the group, for example: Before school lets out in June, and a number of people go off on vacation? In June, on the actual anniversary of the town receiving its charter? In conjunction with the long holiday weekend around the Fourth of July?

The ensuing conversation might sound like this:

CONNIE: So those are some of the options. Who has a preference?

RALPH: I think this is a no-brainer. You need to have the support and involvement of school parents, so the celebration needs to be in early June, at the latest.

BILL: Well, sorry, Ralph, but your own logic argues for the Fourth of July weekend. Everybody's expecting a big party anyway—fireworks and so on—so it makes the most sense to have it then. Believe me, people stick around for that or come back into town for it. Plus, you get two parties for the price of one, which makes a hell of a lot of sense.

VINCE: Excuse me, guys, but I think I'd better speak up for history if no one else is going to.

CONNIE: What do you mean, Vince?

VINCE: It makes absolutely no sense to celebrate the bicentennial on any day other than the bicentennial itself. In other words, on the day of the chartering. I mean, do you guys celebrate your birthday on some random day? Look at what happened when they invented "Presidents' Day" in February. People forgot all about Lincoln and Washington and headed for the malls. My point is that people need to feel a real *connection* to this if it's going to work at all.

SALLY: Speaking as someone who's probably run more fundraisers than anybody else in this room, the thing that *really* matters in terms of dates is not setting up a conflict with some other event. That's what'll kill you, not whether it's the real birthday or not. If you counterprogram against somebody else, you'll split your audience and give the whole effort a bad name.

CONNIE: Molly? Do you want to weigh in?

MOLLY: Not really. Except to say that we'd better give ourselves enough time to pull things together. July sounds a lot easier than May or June. And . . .

CONNIE: And what?

MOLLY: Nothing. Just that if we're going to squabble like this over every little issue, we're not going to get very far.

CONNIE: Good point. And our ground rule is to disagree without being disagreeable. But I like to think that we're not squabbling as much as we're getting interests on the table. As I hear it, we really have four overriding interests that we want to make sure we keep in mind when it comes to picking a date. Molly, since you've agreed to be the recorder, I think it would be good if you jotted them down on the flip chart. And please speak up, folks, if you think I've gotten something wrong, or Molly hasn't recorded it accurately.

    First of all, I think everybody would agree that we want a big turnout, if we're going to put a big effort into this. Second, we want to have people feel historically connected to this thing, whatever it ultimately turns out to be. So we want a date that doesn't conflict with other things, not only to ensure a good turnout but to avoid appearing arrogant or out of touch, and we have to keep our eye on the actual anniversary of the chartering. Third, to the extent that we can get more bang for our buck by piggybacking on other things that are going on, that makes sense. And fourth, we want to do this in a quality way. If we discover that an earlier date doesn't allow for quality, we'll probably want to back off that earlier date.

    Let's keep working on this issue of the date. My sense is that some people feel more strongly about this than others, but we can work something out.

Note how Connie tries to get at the **interests** behind each **position**. Note, too, how she tries to separate each individual from his interest, and how she brings several concerns together into one interest (e.g., turnout). It's not that people are being asked to abandon their interests—which is *never* the goal of consensus building!—but rather, to see their particular interest as part of a bigger picture.

Separate "inventing" from "committing"

An absolutely critical part of CBA is **getting good ideas on the table**, and the more good ideas, the better. Although the process eventually needs to come to an end. The general principle should be to delay making choices as long as possible and to keep generating more good ideas.

Inventing needs to be seen as a "safe" process (which in fact it is). People need to feel free to volunteer ideas that they don't fully endorse, or which the group that they represent might reject. In CBA, no one is ever forced to live with something just because, in the spirit of brainstorming, that person was the only one who said it out loud.

Another piece of the inventing process has to do with packaging options in various ways. Consensus building is a little like bartering in frontier days: When each trading party brought only a limited number of goods to the table, trading was difficult. When each party was able to put all kinds of things on the table, the bargaining was likely to be much more satisfactory to everyone: "I'll trade you this, this, and this for that, that, and that."

The difference in CBA is that **packages are still only options.** They are not put on the table for thumbs-up or thumbs-down votes. Until very late in the dialogue, they are just collections of good ideas, combined and recombined in interesting ways. In packaging, as in brainstorming, **inventing** must be kept separate from asking for **commitments**.

Finally, in the inventing stage, it's helpful to play the game of "What if?" This is simply a way of testing packages, like those frontier traders. "What if I did this, this, and this?" one trader might ask the other. In CBA, it's more likely to take the form of, "What if the group did this, this, and that? Would that meet your concerns? If not, what would have to change to make the package more appealing?" Obviously, the facilitator plays an important part in shaping the what-ifs. Given a good dynamic at the table, though, there's no reason why individual parties can't invent and present their own what-ifs.

Let's eavesdrop on Blaine's Bicentennial Committee (BCC) as it engages in some inventing. Let's assume that the "traditionalist" versus "modernist" issue has heated up a bit. Recall that superintendent Ralph and physician/historian Vince are modernists, meaning that they want to present an unvarnished, educational, warts-and-all version of Blaine's history, whereas volunteer-coordinator Sally and CEO Bill, both traditionalists, want a positive, upbeat, celebration. (Human resource executive Molly hasn't expressed an opinion on this topic.)

Ralph and Vince have proposed that the BCC sponsor a dramatic presentation in the high school auditorium featuring key scenes from Blaine's past. They propose to include, among other more positive things, renditions of a celebrated murder case from the 1890s and a textile-workers' strike from the 1930s. They also want to hire a historian to prepare an accompanying text putting each scene in its historical context; this material would be included as part of the program that would be handed out on the evening of the presentation. Vince has secured a commitment from the Historical Commission to do whatever it takes to make such an event a success . . . at least from a historical perspective.

Beyond that, Ralph is convinced that there are two additional events that are worth serious consideration: a quiz show based on Blaine's history, to be staged in the auditorium and cablecast, and a panel discussion on the future of Blaine. He believes that this sequence of three evening events (including the dramatic presentation) would both capture the town's past and point toward its future.

Bill, meanwhile, has continued to lobby for a parade and fireworks display, preferably to coincide with the town's traditional Fourth of July celebration. He has priced out a more dramatic set of pyrotechnics than usual, as well as some impressive floats for the parade. (Blaine's parades don't normally include much beyond the high school marching band, the VFW, and some politicians.)

Sally, the other traditionalist, has no problem with parades and fireworks, but thinks that a day-long field day and crafts fair, with periodic historical reenactments, would be more to the point. She has inquired about the cost of hiring professional actors to play key figures in Blaine's history. As she sees it, these figures would dress in period costume, talk "in character" to passersby, and occasionally stage a more formal dramatic set piece.

Molly, who still doesn't seem particularly interested in the traditionalist versus modernist arguments, has begun pushing for an upgrade to the town's website. Currently, the site devotes only a paragraph to the history of Blaine. Why not put our time and money into something that will *last*, she asked at a recent meeting, and will be accessible to people all over the world? Why not use a technology that's relatively cheap, unlike print, for example, which our young people are excited about and which would support a continual upgrading and expansion of the project in years to come? She has suggested that she could probably get the necessary programming done at a discount, or perhaps even for free.

At the third meeting of the BCC, in the basement conference room at the town hall, Connie summarizes the various options before the group. Molly writes them on flip charts as Connie talks, and posts them on the wall. Connie opens the discussion as follows:

CONNIE: So it feels to me like we have a lot of ideas on the table.

BILL: Too many.

CONNIE: Why do you say that?

BILL: Well, for one thing, there isn't enough time to do all this stuff. It's one thing to order up three nights of show, and a whole other thing to actually crank out the sausage. I've put on a couple of roasts of prominent people in town, and I'm telling you, it's a huge amount of work. Plus, we can't afford most of this stuff. Let me remind the group that we have an appropriation of only $5,000 from the town. It's obvious that we're going to need private donations.

Frankly, I think some of this stuff will never fly with those kinds of donors. Murders and strikes? Forget it.

SALLY: Right. Absolutely. That's a downer.

VINCE: Well, I'm not so sure that guys walking around in buckskin and tricornered hats between the carnival rides is going to be an easy sell, either. By the way, I'd like someone to explain to me what happens when it rains cats and dogs on the day of your big event. No parade, no crafts in the park, no guys in buckskin, no fireworks. Nothing.

MOLLY: I'm inclined to agree. And just to put in a plug for my own pet project, it never rains on a website.

BILL: Unless your server goes down. Then you've got nothing.

RALPH: Let me just say at this point that I'm certainly not wedded to three successive nights of programs. At previous meetings, people at this table have argued in favor of fun stuff, and also in favor of looking toward the future. If people don't want to bother with the quiz show or the panel discussion, well, fine—that's two fewer things on my plate.

CONNIE: OK. I hear strong opinions being expressed and maybe some frustration. People want to celebrate and they want to educate. People want to party but also to be contemplative. These things don't feel like they're fitting together yet. And at the same time, we all recognize that we can't do everything, given our time and budget constraints.

VINCE: Well, if Molly's with me and Ralph, I'm happy to make a motion that we move ahead on the dramatic presentation at the high school. It would be good to pin at least *one* thing down, and get started on it.

CONNIE: Whoa! Slow down, Vince! We're nowhere near a vote on anything. We're still brainstorming.

VINCE: [*laughs*] Worth a try, anyway.

CONNIE: What I was going to suggest is, let's start thinking about how we can pick a subset of all these ideas, and maybe package them in a couple of ways that still keep you all on board, but are affordable and doable. Does anybody have any ideas in that direction?

BILL: Well . . . maybe we have to start thinking in one of two ways, or maybe two of two ways. First, I guess we have to look at kind of "one from column A; one from column B." Some of what Vince and Ralph are talking about, and some of what Sally and I have been pushing.

Although I don't know exactly what this means, we probably have to look for ways that you get celebration "inside" education, or vice versa. "Two mints in one," as they say.

CONNIE: What would either or both of those things look like?

BILL: Jeez, Connie, I just *said* I didn't know. Maybe you have two nights running—the first night as the indoor thing, and the second night as the outdoor thing. With a rain date for that second night. Maybe it's night-day-night, starting with the serious stuff, running through some of the stuff that Sally's talking about, and winding up with a bang. Literally.

CONNIE: Interesting. Make sure you write down that "night-day-night" phrase, Molly. That's sort of a flow-of-events approach.

VINCE: Well, not to throw Bill's own words back at him, but he's already made the point that we can't afford to do everything.

CONNIE: I'm not sure that's what he's saying, Vince. And in any case, I don't think we should get hung up on the dollars just yet.

What if as we settled on what we think is the right menu of events—which probably doesn't mean everything we've thought of—we also priced them out and then started attaching certain kinds of support to certain kinds of things? I mean, if certain things can only get supported by public dollars, and other things can win private support, shouldn't we look at it that way? At least try it on for size?

VINCE: No harm in that.

BILL: Sounds about right. When it comes to cutting stuff, if we need to, we'll have to be evenhanded.

CONNIE: Right. Meanwhile, I want to get back to the other idea that Bill raised, the "two mints in one" idea. I see that Molly wrote that down, too. Ralph, suppose you had the job of making sure that the dramatic presentation in the high school included a couple of fun, upbeat segments as well as the more serious stuff. Could you do that?

RALPH: Hmmm. Well, I guess we could include some elementary school kids singing songs. Maybe the dance classes at the high school level could put something together. We could even have a segment that was a quiz show looking back at today from the future. I guess I'd want to ask the Drama Club advisor about things like pacing and so on. She knows her stuff. The Blaine Players could also be invited to participate.

CONNIE: Sally, what if some of this more festive stuff also showed up in some form or another during the daytime events?

SALLY: That goes partway toward the sort of things I'd like to see. Not all the way, but partway.

CONNIE: OK. Well, let's keep our eye on that. We need to keep thinking about what's actually involved in the daytime stuff, assuming we go that route.

Molly, we haven't talked much about contemporary technologies—websites and all.

MOLLY: I noticed. I think I'm a minority of one on that issue.

CONNIE: Yeah, but you know what? I work with kids all day long, and I know how much time they spend online. I also know that the website is the first impression that a lot of people elsewhere in the world get of our town. So I'm wondering if there's some way to take the material that Ralph and Vince might generate in connection with the evening presentation and use that as website content.

MOLLY: You mean, like, "scenes from Blaine's past," or whatever?

CONNIE: Sure. What if you were involved in shaping the material that went into the program, or booklet, to make sure that it served the purposes of the website?

MOLLY: Interesting. It might work. Make that historical stuff do double-duty. Actually, if Vince and the Historical Commission were willing, we could probably do a lot more with visuals as well as text, on the website. It's so much cheaper. Plus it's expandable, if the idea catches on and people want to do more of it. You could key people out of the program to the website, you know, "for a longer version, with illustrations, go to www.townofblaine.org" or whatever.

VINCE: I don't want to always be the guy who spits in the soup, but I'm going to keep putting in a plug for *accuracy*. If we have to choose between the truth and what I call "happy talk," I know where I'm going to come down.

CONNIE: Right. Which means that we have to avoid getting to that point. And I think everybody else has a similar sort of bottom line that they don't want to give up, either.

Good work, guys. Why don't I pull together a summary of the kinds of things we've talked about tonight and circulate it before the next meeting?

Create subcommittees and seek expert input

Now that the planners in Blaine seem to be making some progress, let's return to our list of key features of CBA deliberations. In chapter 4, we touched briefly on the use of subcommittees. In addition to delegating the "housekeeping" chores (such as tracking the budget) to qualified individuals, subcommittees can serve as a tool for funneling expert advice into the discussion. We've already made the distinction between **expert witnesses**, who tend to be called to make specific partisan points, and **expert advisors**, who help everybody at the table get up to speed. In many CBA efforts, and especially in very complicated disputes, subcommittees are structured around these expert advisors.

The first step toward setting up effective subcommittees for this purpose is to **formulate a joint fact-finding agenda**. This means, simply, asking and answering a number of questions in advance. For example:

- What facts do we need?
- Who do we agree should do our fact-finding for us?
- What methods do we agree our fact-finders should use?
- What do we agree we should do if there are still gaps or uncertainties at the end of our agreed-upon fact-finding efforts?

The more complicated the issue, the more important a shared base of knowledge is likely to be. A good example is the ongoing debate over fishing off the North Atlantic coast. Environmentalists want to protect what they say are declining fish stocks; fishermen want to protect their livelihood. Consensus building on this difficult subject depends upon the creation of a set of baseline numbers that all parties accept, beginning with the most important fact of all: are fish stocks declining, holding their own, or increasing?

Whose estimates will we all accept as definitive, assuming they use an agreed-upon sampling method over an agreed-upon period of time? Who should be on the boat doing the sampling? Should the sampling procedure change in response to changed environmental conditions— for example, a severe storm that changes the turbidity of the water or otherwise disrupts the local ecological balance? Should fishermen be allowed, or even encouraged, to engage in parallel sampling alongside the "neutral" boat? Who should interpret the results of the sampling, which may not be as conclusive as we hope?

This raises the key concern in selecting experts. As a rule, it makes sense for the consensus-building group to describe what it wants and needs, and then to let the facilitator generate a list of appropriate (and available) candidates for the job. When a candidate is agreed to by all parties, it often makes sense to let that expert "push back" on the definition of the assignment. (The expert is very likely to know something about the topic that the group hasn't factored into its thinking.) It may also make sense at that juncture to agree to a somewhat modified fact-finding assignment. Or, assuming the resources are available, it may make sense to run more than one fact-finding effort in parallel.

This, in turn, raises a third possible role for subcommittees: to **draft summaries of expert opinion**. If there are fifty people in a CBA group, and five experts have assembled extensive data on two or three key points, it's probably unrealistic to think that all fifty people will wade through all the assembled evidence. This is the point when a carefully selected subcommittee—one that represents all the major categories of stakeholders—may want to sit down with the experts and come up with a digest of relevant findings.

It's possible, even likely, that such a subcommittee will come up with alternative interpretations of what they hear. That's perfectly OK (as long as the larger body gets a manageable number of interpretations to consider). In fact, it's better to have a broader range of interpretations— one that is clearly inclusive—than to have a narrow range that may strike somebody as unfairly selective.

One caution at this point: even the best subcommittee can't stand in for the deliberations of the larger group. Sometimes consensus build-ers fall into a trap. They might think: We hired the best experts. They did a great job. Our all-star subcommittee listened hard, did its home-work, and came up with a compelling interpretation. Our job, obvi-ously, is to validate that interpretation.

Not at all. The larger group's job is to continue the excellent work of that outstanding subcommittee and to subject it to what-ifs and other forms of appropriate scrutiny. No expert, or collection of ex-perts, has all the answers, and no subcommittee can substitute for the larger group.

Let's go back briefly to the Bicentennial Committee (BCC), which is in the midst of its deliberations, trying to find a package that will appeal to all parties. At its fourth meeting, the BCC decided to set up two new subcommittees (in addition to its existing Budget Subcom-mittee). Bill dubbed them the "Indoor" and "Outdoor" subcommit-tees, and the names, which had the advantage of being completely neutral, stuck.

The Indoor Subcommittee was charged with the task of finding ways to make the dramatic presentation at the high school both historically accurate and entertaining. Its membership included Vince (a modernist) and Bill (a traditionalist). Molly asked if she could sit in on this subcommittee's meetings, given her interest in a web version of whatever form the presentation ultimately took, and the larger group agreed.

The Outdoor Subcommittee, consisting of Sally (a traditionalist) and Ralph (a modernist), was asked to think through options for the field day/parade/fireworks proposal.

Both groups agreed to forward any cost information to the Budget Subcommittee (Bill and Ralph), as soon as that information became available. Bill and Ralph agreed to prepare a report for the larger group about the likely cost of the whole evolving plan, on the assumption that cost estimates would become more realistic as the individual events came into sharper focus.

Bill, as chairman, calls the meeting to order. After taking care of some housekeeping issues, he turns the gavel over to Connie, who asks the subcommittees to make their reports:

CONNIE: Let's begin with our Indoor experts. Bill or Vince?
BILL: OK. Vince is passing around a summary of our ideas. Long story short, and assuming that we're going to restrict ourselves to one Indoor night, there are a couple of ways to go. One is to go for more or less straight drama. The other is to go for more of a mixed bag. It seems that there are pros and cons to both.

For example, straight drama done right is powerful and educational but also harder to sustain. More time to prepare, and maybe more money, in the sense of possibly having to hire some professional actors or singers to help out. You can't necessarily count on amateurs and school kids to pull it off. The mixed bag, on the other hand, would be fun, but it would have to be different from all the other mixed bags that get put on in our schools—talent shows and so on. It would have to have some content that would lift it out of the ordinary and probably need some input from real theater people.

I have to say that we *did* start seeing some ways that at least some of the money that got spent on the Indoor evening might show up the following day . . . like in the parade. Which of course I support.

CONNIE: Great work. I see Molly has written "straight drama" and "mixed bag" up on the wall, so it looks like Bill has provided us with another set of colorful terms. Anything you want to add, Vince?

VINCE: Nope. Except that I'm working pretty hard to get the Historical Commission comfortable with the "mixed bag," as Bill puts it. They can be a little . . . traditional in their thinking.

CONNIE: Molly? You sat in?

MOLLY: I did. I'm pretty confident that the content that goes into the Indoor activity—whatever that turns out to be—will be adaptable to the website. I went along with Vince to one of the Historical Commission meetings, and I'd agree with his characterization. I think I'll have to do some work to get some of them comfortable with what works on the website, and what doesn't. Like, "shorter is better."

CONNIE: Thanks. And who's reporting from the great Outdoors?

RALPH: That would be me. Basically, as we agreed, Sally and I pushed all the live ideas forward to see where they could go. I have a summary here, too, in a spreadsheet form, and I'll pass that around.

So what you're looking at, down the left-hand side, is our options, and across the top, some pros and cons. If you look at "parade," for example, you can assess it on its own and also see how it might fit into the bigger picture. It's the same with the "field day" and the fireworks.

Maybe the hardest thing we had to figure out was some options for the field day. A whole day is a lot of time to fill.

We came up with a combination of things that I think you'll find interesting. For example, there's a group of guys who dress in old-fashioned baseball outfits, wear handlebar moustaches, and play some old-time version of the game. They'd be willing to dress up as the old Blaine Bees, if we'll provide the jerseys and caps. Other than that, and reimbursement for mileage, they cost nothing. They just like to play old-fashioned baseball.

We've also looked at old-time crafts—carding wool, spinning on a loom, a blacksmith. We're drawing up a list of old-time competitions that kids can participate in, ranging from sports to spelling bees. Apple-bobbing, horseshoe-tossing, and so on.

Fireworks kind of speak for themselves. Everybody likes them, they're associated with celebrations, and Blaine sure knows how to set them off. The only question is, how much can we spend? But fireworks are basically modular—you can always add or take away—so that's a decision we can leave until pretty late in the game.

CONNIE: Sally, do you want to add anything?

SALLY: I think Ralph summed it up fairly, although you'll have to really study the spreadsheet to get the whole picture. I guess I have to admit that my thinking evolved as we looked into this. I gradually started to think that this day of activities, if we actually do it, has to tie into the town's history in meaningful ways. Otherwise, it's just another field day, right?

VINCE: Well, I'm glad you said it, Sally, because I would have if you didn't. I actually *like* the idea of the Blaine Bees playing the Compton Comets, or whoever, as long as we put together a little program that tells people when the Bees got started, why they died out in the '30s, and so on. Nothing fancy, but something with some meat for those who are interested.

I think this raises a bigger question. No offense, Connie, but I think the way you structured this—Indoors, Outdoors—almost guarantees that we'll miss some opportunities to tie everything together. Bill kind of hinted at it. Why couldn't the kids in the Indoors presentation be on a float in the parade, for example?

BILL: Exactly. Two for the price of one.

CONNIE: No offense taken, Vince. I think you guys are definitely headed in the right direction. It sounds like everybody thinks that more integration is better than less integration, so let's keep that in mind as we move forward.

Bill, is it time to talk dollars?

BILL: Well, I have something to hand out, but it's still too early to put real prices on much of anything. In some cases, we're probably just going to have to set a limit and ask people to hold themselves to it. The Indoor presentation, for example, could be anything from custodial overtime to a full-scale Broadway production. Plus, there's some revenue potential there, as well.

As I've said before, we are definitely going to need private support. A good fireworks display alone will run two or three times our entire appropriation. If we want to implement all these great ideas, we're gonna have to start raising money, big time.

CONNIE: We have the problem of things being too ill-defined to put a price on, and yet we know we're going to have to raise some private money. We've already talked about dedicating the public dollars to things that may prove hard to sell privately.

Again, I see good progress, and I hope you see it, too. May I make a process suggestion, at this point? Why don't I touch base with all of you separately and pull together a summary document with some exhibits attached? If at our next meeting we can bless some version of this thing as the outside boundaries on what we're talking about, maybe we can also identify some good targets for fund-raising. Like, maybe the Blaine Bees can get some corporate sponsorship, or the program for the game can be donated by one of the local copy shops.

Obviously, we don't want to get ahead of ourselves. We don't want to have the final lineup determined by what sells and what doesn't. But if we know we want to wind up with some fireworks, and we think that's sellable, maybe we can get started on that kind of thing.

Use a single-text procedure

Connie's wrap-up statement foreshadows the next item on our list: **the use of a single-text to focus deliberations**.

As you can imagine, the end result of all this inventing, packaging, and what-iffing is a blizzard of words. Eventually, someone has to pull the right words (ideas) together in a way that people can use them.

We recommend what's called a "single-text procedure" for this purpose. Rather than inviting each interest group to write up its own proposal, the facilitator needs to create a **single-text**, which blends many points of view into a unified document. This document is then reviewed, debated, and amended by the larger group. Some version of it eventually serves as the focal point for continuing discussions.

How do you get to this important text? Basically, the facilitator meets privately with each constituent group and elicits their sense of the "ideal package." By this point, we hope, the stakeholders have moved somewhat off their opening statements—having learned things through fact-finding and discussion—but they very likely still have distinctive, interest-driven viewpoints. The facilitator generates a single-text, a working summary, after meeting with Group A. She then brings that "clean" draft into a discussion with Group B. She modifies the single-text after hearing from Group B, and then goes off to meet with Group C with a new consolidated text in hand.

Generally, the facilitator doesn't share the multiple drafts along the way. Instead, she finishes a consolidated draft—based on *all* previous meetings—and then takes the consolidated version to the next group for brainstorming. Brainstorming is sometimes done in the larger group, but that can present two kinds of problems. First, it can be inefficient, and second, it can complicate the process by making clear that particular proposals are attributed to certain individuals or groups. If Group A is on record as being opposed to *anything* that Group B likes, then even a great solution may be rejected if it's known to have come from Group B.

Conversely, Group B may have come a long way in its thinking, as a result of the fact-finding and inventing. Maybe its members now see the need to make a break from their earlier ways of thinking, but they don't necessarily want to advertise that fact. Having a single-text circulating, with no attributions, can make the embrace of new ideas easier.

One critical ground rule for the single-text phase is to **withhold criticism, and focus on suggested improvements**. If the group has done its work, and the facilitator has done her part, the single-text should be something that a lot of the members of the larger group will be happy with . . . maybe even delighted. So the challenge becomes, what can we change to bring the nondelighted member(s) aboard without driving anyone away?

Sometimes, late reservations have less to do with the content of the text, and more with things outside the text. Someone may be wondering, legitimately, about what will happen if circumstances change. We all may like this document today, this skeptic may be saying, but what happens if the assumptions behind the document prove wrong? To cite one of the issues that has already cropped up: what if we bet on a nice day, and it rains like crazy?

One way to deal with this kind of concern is to include "contingent options" as part of the package. Different views of the future are played out as *if/then* scenarios. *If* this happens, *then* we agree to do the following. (Depending on the number and complexity of such contingencies, they may be attached to the single-text as an appendix.) This approach almost never upsets others in the group, since they don't believe that any of these unlikely scenarios will ever be played out.

Let's imagine that Connie has talked privately to the five other members of the Blaine Bicentennial Committee, listened to their not-for-attribution comments, and drafted the "single-text" she promised for the next meeting (although she didn't use that particular term). Although time didn't permit the iterative process described above—back to Group A, back to Group B, and so on—she is confident that she has pulled together a useful draft. The resulting document reads as follows:

> The Blaine Bicentennial Committee is charged with planning and implementing the town's upcoming bicentennial celebration, as authorized by the mayor. We are committed to mounting a series of events, within the limits of the public appropriation and whatever private dollars may be raised, which is both festive and educational. We are also committed to documenting these events in ways that will be useful to current and future generations.
>
> We currently anticipate two successive evenings' worth of activities "surrounding" an intervening day of activities. The first evening will consist of a dramatic production, to be staged in the high school auditorium, and will feature a wide range of performers, probably including both professional and nonprofessional actors and singers. Its content is still being worked out, but it will consist of a series of vignettes intended to illuminate and celebrate Blaine's traditions, and also look toward the future. It will combine historical accuracy with appropriate degrees of drama and human interest.
>
> The published program for the evening's entertainment will provide additional historical background for some or all of the vignettes, and will be intended as a significant memento of the bicentennial. Additionally, these written materials will be made available, along with appropriate illustrative materials, for use on an upgraded Blaine municipal website.
>
> The following day's activities will begin with a parade from the town hall to the fairground. Our expectation is that the parade will be of a higher quality than normal and may include floats based in part on the previous evening's presentations. By reusing certain materials, we hope to reach more citizens, and get "more bang for our bucks."
>
> At the fairground, we will offer nearly a full day's worth of educational and fun activities, mostly with an "old-fashioned" theme. These will include

sports and entertainments ranging from relay races to apple-bobbing and horseshoe-tossing, as well as a variety of crafts demonstrations. (If possible, the leaders of these activities will dress in period costumes.) We anticipate running several age-grouped spelling bees, and—if preparation time permits—a Blaine Trivia Game Show. Vendors will be encouraged to sell appropriate foods and beverages, and sponsors will be asked to provide free drinks, prizes, ice cream, etc. One highlight of the afternoon will be an old-fashioned baseball game between the Blaine Bees and a worthy opponent (perhaps the Compton Comets). This event will draw on the services of a group of amateur athletes who stage such events all over the eastern part of the state.

After a break for dinner (and for the sun to set), we will sponsor a high-quality pyrotechnic display, again at the fairgrounds. If the high school marching band (or a similar band) is available, we may intersperse patriotic music with the fireworks.

Blaine's actual "birthday"—the date of chartering—is June 20th, which fortunately falls on a Friday this year. This suggests that our celebrations should be scheduled for Friday evening, the day of Saturday the 21st, and Saturday evening. Our hope is that, with the exception of some early vacationers, most people will still be in Blaine at that time. We should note that holding a significant celebration toward the end of June argues against holding a large-scale Fourth of July celebration in Blaine (i.e., two weeks later). We therefore request that the town reallocate some or all of its Fourth of July celebration budget to the bicentennial celebration.

See the attached budget worksheet.

As an exhibit, Connie attached the Budget Subcommittee's most recent worksheet, which looked like the table on the following page.

Modify the agenda and ground rules as necessary

One good thing about consensus building, and another thing that distinguishes it from Robert's Rules, is that the group can always agree to expand or narrow its agenda or to change its ground rules.

Is it becoming clear that your work needs to expand to include a particular unforeseen concern? Well, expand your scope. (Narrowing your scope is also possible, as long as you don't leave key constituencies behind.) Is something not working from a process point of view?

BUDGET SUBCOMMITTEE WORKSHEET

Event	Item	Expense	Revenue?	Private dollars?
Dramatic presentation	Actors' stipends	1000		
	Sets, etc.	1000		
	Custodial overtime	300		
	Program/memento	4000		Donated printing?
	Gate		1500	
Parade	Floats	2000		Subsidized floats?
	Police overtime	1000		
	Contracted clean-up crew	1000		Donated labor?
Field day/crafts fair	Police overtime	2000		
	Portable toilet rentals	1500		
	Sports equipment	500		
	Baseball-related costs	500		Donated uniforms?
	Contracted clean-up crew	1000		
	Food/beverages		1000	Donated goods?
Fireworks	Contracted pyrotechnics	12000		Subsidized pyros?
Website	Photo scans	500		Donated scans?
	Programming	2000		Subsidized prog?
Publicity	Newspaper	600		Donated ads?
	WBLA radio	400		Donated airtime?
Miscellaneous	Postage	200		
	Photocopies	300		
	Other	1000		
Totals		32800	2500	(to be determined)

Figure out why, and change the ground rule that pertains to that problem. Is Molly proving too partisan, or too lazy, or too fussy to serve as an effective recorder? Move her out, gently—call it a "rotation," rather than a demotion—and move someone else in.

Another issue that falls under this heading is the problem of late arrivals. Sometimes, despite the best efforts of the assessor, the facilitator, and the larger group, a key stakeholder gets left out. (Sometimes you spot them; sometimes they come knocking on your door.) There are no hard and fast rules for responding to late arrivals. It's unlikely that the entire group will be willing to start from scratch, just to accommodate a newcomer. On the other hand, the group has to be willing to spend extra time figuring out the concerns of this latecomer, and find ways to work his or her ideas into the emerging agreement.

Set a hard deadline for ending deliberations

Here's another point that may seem self-evident but needs to be made explicit: **eventually, you have to stop brainstorming.**

There's no yardstick available to determine when you've reached that point. Sometimes there's an external deadline. Sometimes the group agrees in advance that it will hold a specific number of meetings, and no more. (Unless the problem is fully scoped in advance, though, this can be risky!) Often, the group realizes that the single-text isn't going to get any better. This occurs when the last several rounds of brainstorming and elaborating haven't really led to any significant improvements. Sometimes the group simply agrees that it is exhausted, and there's nothing more to be gained from further discussion.

It's helpful to discuss the basis for "completion" in advance: how will we know when we're done? Conversely, it's better *not* to begin this discussion when the group is tapped out.

In Blaine, the Bicentennial Committee began its work with a firm deadline in mind (the June anniversary, or some date close to that). The BCC therefore understood that it would have to complete its deliberations within a limited period. The group also understood that it would have to build into its schedule time for each person at the table to go back to his or her "constituents" and get "buy-ins"—or learn what stands in the way of buy-ins.

After Connie presented the single-text reproduced earlier, the BCC held two more meetings to flesh out the plan and make necessary adjustments, especially in these areas:

- Content of the first evening's dramatic presentation
- Parade participants
- Sports events and featured crafts
- Financial support (i.e., cash donations, sponsorship, discounts, in-kind donations, etc.)

At the group's tenth formal meeting, Connie hands out the latest revised version of the single-text document, which is not significantly different from the one she handed out the previous week. Now, having discussed the subject with chairman Bill in advance, she raises the issue of ending the group's deliberations:

CONNIE: I want to take the group's temperature. It feels to me like we're getting close to wrapping up this phase of our work. Most of the changes from the last round to this one were in the realm of fine-tuning the budgets.

   And to tell you the truth, some of you are looking like I feel—a little tired. I think we'd all like to get our Tuesday nights back.

SALLY: Hear, hear!

MOLLY: I'm all for that.

CONNIE: Ralph? Bill? Vince?

RALPH: I think we're pretty much where we need to be. It's in the nature of things like this to keep evolving right up to show time. I don't think we have to do much more as a group. I think it's time to share the plan with some more people and see what we hear back.

BILL: My only remaining concern at this point is on the funding side. I think we all just about died when we saw that first full budget, showing us more than $30,000 in the hole. The town has helped a lot by throwing in a piece of the Fourth of July budget, and also committing some police and public works department time. A lot of private donors have also come through. So we've got it down to a middle four-figure deficit now—in the $6,000 range—and there are still some potential backers sitting out there. So I'm comfortable.

VINCE: Well, here I go again, but I'm not so comfortable.

CONNIE: What's your concern, Vince?

VINCE: Here's the worst case: we get close to the event, and that $6,000 hole hasn't been closed. What happens then? Somebody has to chop one big thing or lots of little things. Frankly, I don't want *my* favorite stuff chopped, and I'm sure most of you feel the same way. Who's going to do the chopping?

CONNIE: This might be the point to revive the idea of a contingency plan. Suppose we say that the current plan reflects the group's unanimous agreement, contingent upon its being fully funded before the end of the month? If full funding is not available, we will work as a group to figure out exactly how to deal with that situation.

BILL: Sounds good to me. And of course, Ralph and I will keep you posted on our progress in the meantime. Meanwhile, let me say again that I'm confident that the money will be found. The package we've come up with has something for everybody, and that's helping a lot on the fund-raising side.

SALLY: So what are we agreeing to, here? That we're going to take, say, two weeks off while we go out and talk this plan up, and then get back together to discuss what we've heard?

VINCE: Connie, I'm seeing a lot of heads nodding around to table. So will you finally let me make a motion to put something to a vote?

CONNIE: [*laughs*] Yes, I think your time has finally come, Vince!

By a show of hands, the group formally endorses the plan, including the contingency described by Connie, and the plan for reconvening in two weeks that has been advocated by Sally. Vince will take the plan back to the Historical Commission, Ralph with check off with the school community, Sally will communicate with her volunteer networks and the African-American community, Bill will touch base both with the mayor's office and the business community, and Molly will talk with members of the high-tech and young professional constituencies.

Build on prior relationships

This building-block in our list of eight features of successful deliberation could just as easily have come first. In many cases, CBA is driven by relationships. It's important to understand relationships and build upon them.

Sometimes relationships are in place before CBA begins. Sometimes the people in Groups A and B have worked together extensively in the past, and there is a foundation of trust to build upon (or of distrust to overcome). If Groups A and B are prepared to "run down the road" together, the facilitator should take full advantage of that—making sure, meanwhile, that Groups C and D aren't left in the dust.

Another way of looking at relationships is to ask, "Who's going to be working with whom at the *end* of the process?" When the members of Groups A and B know they will be working at close quarters for the foreseeable future, they tend to act differently at the table. Again, a skilled facilitator takes this kind of forward commitment into account.

One common misconception is that having old buddies at the table makes CBA easier, and having sworn enemies at the table makes it harder. That's sometimes true, but it's sometimes *not* true. Sometimes hearing clear and diametrically opposed opening statements makes participants take the process more seriously. Sometimes this is the first real opportunity for old foes to work together—and good things can come from that.

Relationships can be powerful. And as we will see in chapter 6, sometimes they *need* to be powerful, in order to survive the pressures inherent in the final stages of consensus building.

Emphasize mutual gain

This theme, of course, runs through most of the chapters of this book and it opens the next chapter, so it only needs underscoring here.

CBA is about drawing on the creativity of the group to find better solutions for **all members of the group**. Some people—raised on zero-sum, my-gain-is-your-loss bargaining—initially have a hard time buying this concept, even as they sit down at the table. They start the consensus-building process with skepticism: How can we possibly all come out ahead? How can there not be a loser?

Experience shows, however, that if the conditions are right, mutual gain is there to be found. What conditions? As noted earlier, the challenge at hand has to be "big" enough to allow trades across issues. (Not compromises—**trades**.) The process needs to be managed with skill. The necessary resources have to be in hand. And perhaps most important, people have to be willing to suspend disbelief and invest their time and energy in the process. When they do, and when they follow this and the other steps explained in this book, CBA *works*.

There are a great many success stories we could tell. There are lots of ad hoc groups that have switched to consensus building and, in so doing, avoided personality clashes and sidestepped other wasteful organizational dynamics. There are municipalities that have switched from the traditional "hearings model" to collaborative processes—built around the basics of CBA described in this book—that have been able to site controversial facilities, make difficult budgetary cutbacks, and alter long-standing public policies that many felt, at least at the outset, should not have been changed. There are instances in which national policy-making has operated along CBA lines (even in Congress, where bipartisan efforts have occasionally blossomed because there was too much at stake to do otherwise). There have been global efforts in which CBA has displaced the usual North-South or East-West bickering, as in 1992, when the Rio Summit on Environment and Development produced Climate Change and Biodiversity Protection treaties signed by almost every nation in the world.

The reason that these efforts succeeded (and you can read more about them in the *Consensus Building Handbook* as well as the other books listed in appendix G), is that the participants committed to pursue their own interests in ways that created the possibility of everyone coming out ahead, that is, everyone achieving an outcome better than what they would most likely have gotten if no agreement had been reached. Substantive agreements were achieved because the parties adopted a problem-solving mind-set, deliberated in a nonjudgmental fashion, relied on joint fact-finding, and used a variety of brainstorming and value creation techniques to generate trades (or packages). They didn't do these things for altruistic reasons; they switched to CBA because they realized it was in their own and their group's best interest to do so.

Key Terms and Concepts Explained in Chapter 5
(For further clarification, see Part 2:
The Five Essential Steps in the
Consensus Building Approach, step 3, page 176)

Building a problem-solving mind-set
Deliberating in a nonjudgmental fashion
Separating inventing from committing
Using subcommittees
Joint fact-finding
Summaries of expert opinion
Using a single-text procedure
Modifying the agenda and ground rules as you go
Setting deadlines
Building on prior relationships
Emphasizing the goal of mutual gain

6

∾

Confirming that Agreement
Has Been Reached

Up to this point, most of what we've been describing, both in general terms and in our Blaine example, has been about how to **create value through deliberation**. The members of the Blaine Bicentennial Committee, for example, have built upon each other's interests to create options that otherwise wouldn't have been possible. They have finished the difficult step of coming up with a package, and they are on the verge of deciding on a final version of that package, based on what they hear back from their respective constituencies.

So is their work complete?

In a word, no.

Creating value is only one aspect of consensus building. Equally important is the process of **distributing value**. The consensus builders have planted an orchard, and it is now bearing fruit. If they have done their job well, they already have a good idea of how the fruit will be divvied up among the known constituencies. What happens, though, if people within those constituencies disagree with this tentative distribution of the fruit (the "value")? What happens if new constituencies pop up and argue that they, too, should be in on the spoils?

This is sometimes the hardest part of CBA. The group has worked for weeks or months to reach agreement on a hard-won plan of action. Now its members have to go out and explain the plan to the people they represent, most of whom weren't at the table and have little or no idea of how the tentative plan was constructed. Some of these people may make very tough demands, which their representatives will be obligated to take back to the full group. This tends to create confusion and suspicion: *Why is Vince trotting out all those old arguments again? I thought we settled that question weeks ago. If Vince is going for another bite of the apple, well, so will I!*

Here's where the facilitator really earns her stripes. She has to assess the altered landscape, and keep pushing for ways to keep all the interested parties on board. She has to keep pushing for unanimity but settle for what we call "overwhelming agreement." Or, in the worst case, the facilitator has to admit that the group is unable to reach consensus.

This is the process of **deciding**. In this chapter, we'll highlight three techniques for getting to a fair and overwhelmingly appealing solution. As you will see, they are to some degree an extension and intensification of the processes begun during group problem solving:

- Maximize joint gains
- Keep the record straight
- Anticipate the problems of following through

We will also throw a few curve balls at our friends on the Blaine Bicentennial Committee and see how well they do when, under pressure, they have to redistribute the value that they have created (and meanwhile create more value).

Maximizing joint gains

In a sense, this point is a restatement of much of what you've encountered in previous chapters. Why have we gone through all these meetings, and listened to all these arguments, and set up all these subcommittees, and invented all these options and packages? The answer is, to **maximize joint gains**. In other words, to do better by working together than any of the parties could have done on our own.

As noted at the end of chapter 5, most people approach CBA with their Robert's Rules hat on. Why? Because for the most part, their prior experience has been in a "zero-sum" world in which their gain was someone else's loss and vice versa. This is a world in which you count noses ahead of time, put the question to a vote when you're pretty sure you have enough noses, and go home a winner. In that world, you don't worry about disaffected minorities. After all: we live in a democracy, and they *lost*.

In CBA, the facilitator works hard to overcome a zero-sum mindset. At every opportunity, he points to the evidence that brainstorming, packaging, what-iffing, and all the other techniques of consensus building are actually adding up to joint gains.

In many cases, the facilitator has to come up with analogies that "speak" to the people at the table. Sports buffs understand that a great trade can make both teams better. Stamp collectors know that a great trade can make both collections better. The facilitator has to find the right language, foreshadow what "success" is going to look like, and help the group figure out the steps it can take to get there.

Meanwhile, of course, the group has to produce the goods. When it comes to consensus building, people don't just *accept* the idea of a mutually advantageous outcome. They only embrace it—and as a rule, they *do embrace it*—once trading across issues begins to suggest that interesting packages are possible.

Now let's fast-forward to the juncture when the consensus builders come back from the field to report on what they've heard about the fruits of their discussions; in other words, after a tentative agreement has been circulated among various stakeholders but before the final decision has been made. This is often a very tough moment. People often start restating themes that emerged months before. They deliver what may sound like ultimatums to the group: *If my constituency doesn't get X, Y, and Z, we're walking.*

Here's where the lessons learned and the relationships forged over previous weeks and months are put to the test. The facilitator has to intensify the process of packaging, and repackaging, with an eye toward maximizing joint gains. Here's where he asks, after putting a modified package on the table: "Who can't live with this?"

When someone raises a hand in response to this question, the facilitator must then ask the next question involved in maximizing joint gains: "Well, what's your suggestion for enhancing or embellishing the package in order to make it something you could live with?"

The facilitator (often in real time) summarizes whatever enhancements are proposed by the objecting parties, restates the package in a way that builds these enhancements in, and goes back to his or her first question: "Now, who can't live with this?"

This time, not surprisingly, different hands may go up. Again, the facilitator asks the objecting parties not to state their objections but to propose the change(s) that would make the revised package acceptable. Again, he or she lays out a revised package, and asks, "Who can't live with this?"

Note that the facilitator is taking a pretty active role here. As the group approaches the moment of decision, it may well need this kind of strong hand at the helm. In response to a particular demand, the facilitator may well say, "I don't think we can go there, because adopting what you're proposing means we'd lose too many other people." Or, the facilitator may put three packages on the table and ask for a straw poll: not a *binding* vote but a show of hands to determine the distribution of opinions.

Skilled facilitators begin this process as soon as possible and repeat it as often as necessary. They test and probe, measuring the breadth and depth of support for an emerging package. They make sure that as many options as possible are considered. (Putting all the options in play, or at least as many as possible, is the only way to maximize joint gains.) They seek improvements while also working hard to prevent the latest iteration from driving anyone away.

Trouble in Blaine

At its most recent meeting, as you'll recall from chapter 5, the Bicentennial Committee (BCC) agreed to spend two weeks circulating its single-text document among various constituencies in town. Let's tune in as the group reconvenes after those two weeks. Bill calls the meeting to order, and Connie opens the floor for discussion:

> **CONNIE:** So. What are we hearing out there? Anyone? Nobody's looking very happy tonight. What's going on?
>
> **BILL:** Well, hell, I'll go first. You want it with the bark on, or the bark off?
>
> **CONNIE:** Excuse me?
>
> **BILL:** An old country saying. You can get your bad news with the bark on—meaning, sugar-coated—or with the bark off. Either way.
>
> **CONNIE:** Well, then, I think we need it with the bark off. Bad news?
>
> **BILL:** Yeah, I'd say so. The mayor says he's not going to support our proposal in its current form.
>
> **SALLY:** Oh, great! Dead on arrival.
>
> **CONNIE:** "In its current form," you said. Did he suggest what it would take to make it acceptable?
>
> **BILL:** Sure. And in no uncertain terms. He wants Saturday morning devoted to speech-making by politicians. Including himself. He wants a podium, a speaker's platform, ribbon-cutting, and so on. The whole nine yards. "Especially if you're proposing to kill my Fourth of July holiday," is the way he put it.
>
> **SALLY:** Saturday morning? So everybody else's favorite idea gets left alone, but half of my field day gets turned over to long-winded politicians? I don't think so!
>
> **CONNIE:** Hold that thought, Sally. Let's get other reactions from the world out there before we react to any specific response.

SALLY: Well, fine. I've got some more reactions, if you want to hear them.

CONNIE: That's what we're here for.

SALLY: A number of African Americans have let me know that they're not going to tolerate what they call the "whitewashing" of Blaine's history. They have organized themselves into a group and are demanding the right to march in the parade. They also want to set up a booth at the field day where they're planning to hand out literature. They want to detail the oppression of Blaine's minority communities, including two celebrated lynchings from the '20s.

BILL: Oh, God! Is that going to be the theme of their parade float, too? The "Blaine Hanging Tree"? I'll tell you something; the mayor's gonna *love* that!

SALLY: Wait a minute! I didn't say *I* liked it. I never wanted *any* of this historical muckraking. All I'm doing is telling you what I'm hearing. And by the way, Bill: that tree is part of *your* history, too, whether you like it or not.

VINCE: What the hell happened to the idea of quality control? I mean, up to now, we've been talking about drawing on the Historical Commission to generate the historical materials that will be used in these events. So now what? Now we're going to let any bunch of crackpots hand out whatever slapdash stuff they like?

SALLY: Oh, so your assumption is that because black people are putting it together, it's necessarily going to be—what did you call it?—"slapdash"?

VINCE: Oh, great. So now I'm a *racist* physician and a *racist* historian. Don't tell my black patients. Or my black colleague on the Historical Commission. They wouldn't understand.

CONNIE: Whoa, guys. No one's calling anybody names, here. Let's continue with our debriefing. Vince, what's the Historical Commission thinking about our package?

VINCE: Well, up to about five minutes ago, I would have said we were in good shape. Now I'm not so sure. We're not putting our seal of approval on anybody's hanging tree, I can tell you that.

CONNIE: Uh, I'm going to remind everybody that our number one ground rule is that we disagree without being disagreeable. Let's keep going. Ralph, what are you hearing from the schools?

RALPH: Well, nothing as dramatic as what other people are hearing. Several of my teachers and administrators came to me with an idea for a time capsule. Actually, it's a strong educational concept, and I'm surprised I didn't think of it myself. I guess there's some minor expense associated with it, mainly in preparing and closing up the ground, but I can't think of any other downside. So I hope this group will be open to it.

One other possible wrinkle is that we may have trouble mixing union actors and amateurs on the stage on Friday night. We're seeking a waiver from the Theatrical Guild. If that doesn't come through, we're back to using all amateurs, and some of our more challenging material may be hard to pull off.

VINCE: Great. So now it's not just the parade and the field day that are screwed up, it's *everything*. Friday night is going to be second graders in paper hats waving sparklers. Saturday is going to be speechifying politicians. Maybe we should just bail. Let someone else run this damn party.

CONNIE: Hold it, hold it! Nobody's allowed to throw in the towel just yet. Molly, you've been trying to take notes on all this troubling news. Why don't you put down your markers for a minute and tell us about the status of the website?

MOLLY: Mmm, sure, Connie. I'm actually feeling pretty positive about the proposed website upgrade. I'm getting good responses from a group of people who don't normally get involved in town affairs. They all seem willing to work with the Historical Commission to create something pretty special. I think we can do it more or less for free, too.

I have to say I'm troubled by what I'm hearing around this table. Are we really just going to throw all our hard work out the window because people are pushing back on us? Aren't we committed to seeing this thing through?

SALLY: Oh, please. No lectures, Molly. Your little website is the only piece of this that's not getting screwed up.

MOLLY: Well, actually, it sounds like the fireworks are still in good shape. I thought I was supposed to say what I *thought*, Sally, while we're sitting at this table.

CONNIE: You're right. You are. So now we've heard from everybody. I suggest we . . .

BILL: Connie, can I make one more point? A process point?

CONNIE: Sure.

BILL: While the mayor was reaming me out for not including a speakers' segment on Saturday, he made something else pretty clear to me. He said that we're really only an advisory committee and at the end of the day, he's going to make the final call.

VINCE: And your point is . . . ?

BILL: My point is that when you think about it, he's absolutely right. The mayor asked us for help. But at the end of the day, it *is* his call. We're only helping him out.

At the same time, I for one feel like we have to solve this problem for him. I'm not gonna be happy telling him we came up short. And you know what? I actually think we've come up with some good ideas. I'd hate to see all this stuff fall apart at the last minute. I mean, the town deserves the benefit of all the work we've done. And the mayor deserves some success for putting his trust in us.

MOLLY: I think Bill raises an interesting point, and it's one we have to acknowledge. We've been talking about all this stuff like it's *ours*. The fact is, it really belongs to everybody. We can state our preferences, but we can't really shut other people out, right? If the people that Sally was talking about want to march in the parade or set up a booth, we can't really keep them out, right?

SALLY: I guess at the end of the day, I'd argue that we *shouldn't* keep them out.

VINCE: All I'm saying is that the Historical Commission isn't going to put its seal of approval on things it has zero control over. Believe me. That's a nonstarter.

The conversation continues in this vein for quite a while. Connie tries to draw out everyone's interests, while minimizing the extent to which they rehash old positions or disagree in disagreeable ways. Molly takes notes on the flip charts, tearing the pages off and posting them on the wall as she goes. Occasionally, someone asks for a revision to a word or phrase in Molly's notes, which Connie almost always approves.

When Connie feels that the discussion is pretty much played out, she announces that she wants to try to move the discussion forward. She explains what she means:

CONNIE: I've been reviewing Molly's notes as you've been talking, and I've been trying to tease out the common themes, as well as what appear to be the non-negotiables. Let me put a somewhat revised package on the table, and you guys tell me what you think.

Suppose we agree to include a speakers' segment in the Saturday proceedings. From what Bill says, this is pretty much a non-negotiable from the mayor's office. Let's face it: he may be anticipating pressure from other people, and he may be bowing to the inevitable.

Suppose we put Ralph's time capsule in that segment as well. Let the mayor, or somebody else, officiate over that piece of it. That will give the politicians another thing to do that's not just another speech, which I know Sally isn't real interested in. Could everybody live with that?

SALLY: I still don't like that fact that Saturday is getting taken over by a bunch of windbags.

CONNIE: I know. So maybe we have to think about ways to beef up Friday night, especially in light of what Ralph told us about the Theatrical Guild, and then tie that into Saturday.

What if we could find somebody who could be a serious centerpiece of the Friday night show and also show up in the Saturday speakers' program? Like, a senior citizen who lived through a lot of these years and could tie a lot of things together?

VINCE: Interesting. Somebody who could combine the education and entertainment themes.

CONNIE: Could everybody live with that?

VINCE: Well, yeah, except that you haven't dealt with the issue of the hanging tree.

SALLY: Oh, for goodness sake . . .

CONNIE: Come on, Vince; we're still working together here. As Bill and Molly have pointed out, we really don't have the authority to say no to people who want to do their own thing in the context of the bicentennial.

Why don't we try looking at this a little differently? Why don't we say that our package comprises the *official* activities—sanctioned by the town, the Historical Commission, the school department, or whoever—and that anyone else is welcome to do their own thing? Meaning, they can march at the back of the parade or set up a booth in the lobby at the high school auditorium or at the fairgrounds, maybe in a specially designated area, but they're on their own. All we'd ask of them is to describe the location and duration of their activity, so that we can include it in the master schedule.

Could everybody live with something like that?

VINCE: So the Historical Commission's name isn't going on these kinds of unofficial activities? That would be perfectly clear?

SALLY: More important: *our* names aren't being lent to things we have no control over. I mean, if some Aryan Nation group shows up on our doorstep, it's not "brought to you by the Blaine Bicentennial Committee"?

BILL: I heard you say the *back* of the parade, right?

CONNIE: Exactly. Can everybody live with that?

MOLLY: Can I make another suggestion?

CONNIE: Please do.

MOLLY: It seems to me that we should make an effort to *welcome* these self-nominating groups. We could do it in the context of the website. In my experience, sometimes people just want to be heard. They just want to be acknowledged.

Now, I don't know these people that Sally is talking about, or the next three groups that may step forward. But suppose we make a real effort to draw them into the website in some way or another? We could make a point of distinguishing between the "official" stuff and the "unofficial" stuff. For some people, that might be enough. They'd get to say their piece in a relatively painless way.

BILL: That would certainly be an unexpected side benefit of the whole website idea.

CONNIE: Thanks, Molly. I'm hearing you offering to welcome outside groups in a constructive way through the vehicle of the website. Maybe those groups would also choose to march in the parade or set up a booth on the fairgrounds, or maybe they wouldn't. That would be entirely up to them.

I have to ask again: can everybody live with what they've heard?

VINCE: I'll say yes, provisionally. If you write up something that captures what we've talked about tonight, I can get behind it.

BILL: Me, too.

SALLY: Provisionally, yes.

RALPH: I have what I need.

MOLLY: Sure.

CONNIE: OK, then, I'll do that tomorrow, using Molly's notes on tonight's meeting, and circulate it first thing Thursday morning. I'll also include the latest figures from the Budget Subcommittee, which Ralph and Bill tell me are looking pretty good.

RALPH: Not just pretty good, *extremely* good. I wish I had Bill's golden touch in the business community. It looks like we won't even have to deplete the Fourth of July account.

CONNIE: Well, that's something to celebrate, right?

Listen, guys: you did some really good work tonight. Please review carefully the document I send you later this week. If you're comfortable with it, consider sharing it with some of those groups we've discussed tonight. For example, Bill, you might want to run it by the mayor if you both have time.

Let's plan on making our final decision next Tuesday night. My goal, as always, is to get a unanimous agreement. If you have problems or suggestions based on what you read, please call me ahead of time so I can bring them to the table on Tuesday.

BILL: Before we call it a night, I just want to add my personal thanks for everybody's hard work—both tonight, and leading up to tonight. I wasn't so sure an hour ago, but I think we may make it to the end zone after all. Hearing no objection, let's adjourn until next Tuesday at 7:00 p.m.

Keeping the record straight

In previous chapters, we have talked about the importance of the note-taking function. When documenting the real-time discussion, the recorder has to be reasonably skilled at capturing its essence in key words or phrases. He has to be seen as unbiased as a recorder—not necessarily unbiased in the deliberations—and has to perform the recording function in an unobtrusive way. If the group has concerns about putting the recording function in the hands of a "partisan," it may want to consider rotating the recorder's job on some prearranged schedule. Similarly, if a recorder starts to look burned out, the group should not hesitate to move a fresh person into that position.

As noted earlier, specific comments should *not* be attributed to individuals, either in the real-time notes, in the meeting summaries, or in the single-text document. If a point of unanimous or general agreement is reached, that should always be documented. If someone takes a strong exception to that agreement, the dissenting opinion should also be recorded, in a nonattributed way: "One objection to Conclusion X was as follows," or words to that effect.

Meeting summaries should be circulated to all participants as soon as possible after each meeting, in a way that doesn't make any individual go through impossible hoops. (E-mail is easy, for example, but not everyone has easy access to e-mail, and sometimes servers go down.) The group should be asked to sign off on these summaries, either electronically or at the beginning of the next meeting. They should also be advised that the collection of meeting summaries will become a useful tool in the "deciding" phase. For example, they may be challenged by a constituent group to explain how a particular decision was reached. Or, they may simply want to make sure that nothing important has fallen off the table over the weeks or months of discussion.

Finally, the notes and summaries of the meetings leading up to the final decision can be critically important as a tool for reviewing the evolving single-text. Did the facilitator get it right?

Let's look at the revised document that Connie produced for the Blaine Bicentennial Committee. If you compare it to the version presented in chapter 5, you'll see some subtle but important changes:

The Blaine Bicentennial Committee is charged with advising the Mayor's Office on the planning and implementation of the town's upcoming bicentennial celebration, as authorized by town meeting and the mayor. We are committed to mounting a series of events, within the limits of the public appropriation and whatever private dollars may be raised, that is both festive and educational. We are also committed to documenting these events in ways that will be useful to current and future generations.

We currently anticipate two successive evenings' worth of activities "surrounding" an intervening day of activities. The first evening will consist of a dramatic production, to be staged in the high school auditorium, and will feature a wide range of performers, probably including both professional and nonprofessional actors and singers. Its content is still being worked out, but it will consist of a series of vignettes intended to illuminate and celebrate Blaine's traditions and also look toward the future. It will combine historical accuracy with appropriate degrees of drama and human interest.

The program for the evening's entertainment will provide additional historical background for some or all of the vignettes, and it will be intended as a significant memento of the bicentennial. Additionally, these written materials will be made available—along with appropriate illustrative materials—for use in an upgraded Blaine municipal website.

The following day's activities will begin with a parade from the town hall to the fairground. Our expectation is that the parade will be of a higher quality than normal and may include floats based in part on the previous evening's presentation. By reusing certain materials, we hope to reach more citizens and get "more bang for our bucks." Working with the mayor's office, we will determine the order of march in the parade, with unofficial groups (see below) being welcomed at the end of the parade.

At the fairground, we anticipate nearly a full day of activities. These will begin with (short) speeches by appropriate town and state leaders. We hope to include a speech by a featured speaker who will also have played a role in the dramatic presentation of the previous evening. The mayor and other public officials will ceremonially "bury" a time capsule, to be unearthed on the occasion of Blaine's three hundredth anniversary. We anticipate that a citizen's committee, including but not limited to schoolchildren, will take responsibility for determining the contents of the time capsule. (Actual burial of the capsule, which requires earth-moving equipment, will occur subsequently.)

For the balance of the day, we will offer a range of educational and fun activities, mostly with an "old-fashioned" theme. These will include sports and entertainment ranging from relay races to apple-bobbing and horse-shoe-tossing, and also a variety of crafts demonstrations. (If possible, the leaders of these activities will dress in period costumes.) We also antici-pate running several age-grouped spelling bees, and—if preparation time permits—a Blaine Trivia Game Show. Vendors will be encouraged to sell appropriate food and beverages, and sponsors will be asked to provide free drinks, prizes, ice cream, etc. One highlight of the afternoon will be an old-fashioned baseball game between the Blaine Bees and a worthy oppo-nent (perhaps the Compton Comets). This event will draw on the services of a group of amateur athletes who stage such events all over the eastern part of the state.

After a break for dinner (and for the sun to set), we will sponsor a high-quality pyrotechnic display, again at the fairgrounds. If the high school marching band (or a similar band) is available, we may intersperse patri-otic music with the fireworks.

Blaine's actual "birthday," the date of chartering, is the twentieth of June, which fortunately falls on a Friday this year. This suggests that our celebra-tions should be scheduled for Friday evening, the day of Saturday the twenty-first, and Saturday evening. Our hope is that, with the exception of some early vacationers, most people will still be in Blaine at that time. We should note that holding a significant celebration toward the end of June argues against holding a large-scale Fourth of July celebration in Blaine (i.e., two weeks later).

The Blaine Bicentennial Committee is an ad hoc advisory board. Our role is advisory in nature. As such, we have developed an official program of activi-ties, subject to the mayor's approval. At the same time, we recognize the fact that other groups may seek to be involved in the celebration of the bicenten-nial. While we will not lend the official sanction of the Committee—or the sanction of other contributing bodies, such as the Historical Commission and the school department—to these unofficial groups, we are committed to helping them celebrate the bicentennial in their own way. We will make every effort to represent their points of view in our upgraded website and otherwise suggest ways for them to involve themselves in the town's larger celebration. They will be welcomed at the end of the order of march in the parade and at a specially designated area of the fairground.

See the attached budget worksheet, revised to reflect (1) all town subsi-dies, (2) all private donations, and (3) the $5,000 town meeting appro-priation. As the worksheet makes clear, our proposal has been constructed on a break-even basis, with a small ($1,000) contingency to offset any short-falls in gate receipts or profits on the sale of food and beverages.

REVISED BUDGET WORKSHEET

Event	Item	Expense	Revenue	Source
Dramatic presentation	Actors' stipends	1000		
	Sets, etc.	1000		
	Custodial overtime	300	300	Donated by schools
	Program/memento	4000	4000	Donated printing
	Gate		1500	
Parade	Floats	2000	2000	Subsidized privately
	Police overtime	1000	1000	Donated by town
	Contracted clean-up crew	1000	1000	Donated by town
Speeches/ceremony	AV system rental	1000	1000	Donated privately
	Stage/bunting/banners	1000		
	Time capsule site prep	500	500	Donated privately
Field day/crafts fair	Police overtime	2000	2000	Donated by town
	Portable toilet rentals	1500		
	Sports equipment	500		
	Baseball-related costs	500	500	Donated privately
	Contracted clean-up crew	1000		
	Food/beverages		1000	
Fireworks	Contracted pyrotechnics	12000	12000	5000 reallocated from 7/4 budget
				7000 donated privately
Website	Photo scans	500	500	Donated privately
	Programming	2000	2000	Donated privately
Publicity	Newspaper	600	600	Donated privately
	WBLA radio	400	400	Donated privately
Miscellaneous	Postage	200		
	Photocopies	300		
	Contingency	1000		
BCC appropriation			5000	
Totals		35300	35300	

Anticipate the problems of following through

Our last technique for getting to a fair and overwhelmingly appealing solution can be summarized in the phrase, "anticipate the problems of following through." Note the emphasis: we're not talking about the **content** of the decision but the **process** by which it is reached and subsequently publicized.

The Blaine Bicentennial Committee has anticipated an important problem and dealt with it effectively: the issue of the *advisory* nature of the group's role. CBA in the public sector almost always leads to advisory opinions, which must then be turned over to the individual or group with the formal authority to make and implement such decisions. Some people think this undercuts the importance of consensus building. We argue that the opposite is true: because no one will be compelled to embrace negotiated solutions, it's that much more important to get them right and make sure they are overwhelmingly appealing.

So, in many CBA processes, the stakeholder representatives work to produce an agreement that is then delivered to the convener. It is the convener's decision whether or not to take the proposal forward. There are instances, however, like a board of directors meeting of a not-for-profit corporation, where the product of the CBA is, in fact, a final decision. In those circumstances, the process of reaching agreement (and checking with constituents) is exactly the same. The process of following through, however, does not require checking back with constituents. The participants in these definitive CBA efforts may nevertheless be concerned about how those who are not present will react to what they have decided.

Another issue that comes under the heading of following through when the CBA produces a proposal is the question of **precedent**. Especially in a context that involves organized labor, formal agreements have to be scrutinized for their precedent-setting potential. In some cases, the group may decide to state formally that "this agreement, reached by the such-and-such group in such-and-such a context, is not intended to serve as a precedent in any subsequent circumstance."

Finally, the agreement should be constructed in a way that gives it the best possible chance of being implemented successfully. (Implementation is the subject of our next chapter.) Some mechanism for dispute resolution needs to be built into the agreement. We use the phrase "nearly self-enforcing" to capture the essence of this point. The agreement should include a sentence or paragraph, somewhere near the end, that says something like, "If during the course of implementing this agreement, someone has a problem with what's going on, here's how we propose to handle it." This is the most effective way to hold people to the agreements that lie behind the document.

At the next meeting of the Blaine Bicentennial Committee, Connie explained the issues of precedent-setting and self-enforcement. The group agreed to add language at the end of the document that asserted that this process was not intended to be precedent-setting, and established a mechanism for dispute resolution during the implementation phase.

Then, by a show of hands, the group unanimously endorsed the agreement. After the meeting adjourned, Bill and Vince lingered at the table with Connie. Let's tune in again:

BILL: Well, Connie, you pulled it off.

CONNIE: We all pulled it off, Bill. By the way: there's still a long way to go before your fireworks actually get set off!

BILL: Based on the mayor's reaction to your revised draft, I don't see any problem. And if somebody comes out of the woodwork, I think we've set up ways to deal with that.

VINCE: I wanted to congratulate you too, Connie. I also wanted to say that something really *struck* me tonight about this process. Which is that as you may have noticed, I'm always one for getting the facts on the table and voting, based on those facts. The vote has always seemed to me to be the most important thing. Tonight's vote felt like an afterthought, almost.

CONNIE: Right. Because it was mainly a ratification of what you had already worked so hard to reach agreement on. It wasn't intended to identify winners and losers. It was a way to present a united front to the world.

Just as deliberation is the front porch to decision making, decision making is the front porch to implementation. As Connie pointed out to Bill, simply getting to a decision—even a unanimous one—is not necessarily the end of CBA. (There may be some fireworks *before* the fireworks!) In many cases, the consensus builders will be called upon to make the agreement work, and that is the focus of our next chapter.

Key Terms and Concepts Explained in Chapter 6
(For further clarification see Part 2:
The Five Essential Steps in the
Consensus Building Approach, step 4, page 181)

Creating and distributing value
Maximizing joint gains
Keeping the record straight
Signing off on written summaries
The advisory nature of CBA results
Anticipating the problems of follow-through

7

~

Crafting "Nearly Self-enforcing" Agreements

Getting to a plan, and reaching tentative agreement on that plan, is most of the way toward successful consensus building. In many cases, though, it's not all the way. The consensus-building group still has to worry about challenges during the **implementation phase** of the process. Briefly stated, the group has to anticipate potential obstacles to implementation, and build into their agreement ways for responding to those obstacles. Otherwise, the agreement may be too brittle to hold up under pressure.

Put more positively, the group has to make sure that their agreement is robust, so that when the inevitable pressures come to bear, the agreement is up to the challenge. We use the phrase "nearly self-enforcing" to describe such an agreement. In other words, the package should be structured in such a way that all the constituent groups would rather see it succeed than fail. They don't need some superior authority rapping their knuckles to make them keep their promises. They are all pulling in the same direction, because they know that's where their own best interests lie. And since no one can predict the future with any certainty, each agreement has to provide ways for people to get back together and fix the agreement if and when the unexpected happens.

Steps for creating a robust, "nearly self-enforcing," agreement include:

1. Holding representatives responsible for checking back with their constituents
2. Holding representatives responsible for signing, and committing to, a final agreement in their own name
3. Making sure that the informal becomes formal; in other words, existing legal, regulatory, or administrative mechanisms are activated to turn the advisory group's recommendation into a formal, "legitimized" action
4. Designing appropriate monitoring procedures

Additionally, people who have participated in a successful consensus-building process may want to take steps to evaluate the lessons they have learned, and they want to make sure that those lessons are communicated in ways that will make them available to future consensus builders.

We will look at each of these steps in turn. First, let's look at the psychology of the final stages of the CBA process.

Burn-out and defensiveness: two threats to implementation

There are a number of psychological dynamics that can come into play as the consensus-building process nears completion. Two of the most common negative factors are **burn-out** and **defensiveness**.

Burn-out tends to occur when the members of a group of well-meaning volunteers start to feel as if they've been called upon to do far more than they ever expected to do. Imagine that they have been meeting every Tuesday night for three months. They have slugged and battled their way to a provisional agreement, and this has taken an emotional toll. With the solution seemingly at hand, they may feel like they've earned the right to put down their CBA burden and get on with their lives.

What are the warning signs of burn-out? More or less what you'd expect: crankiness, a willingness to rush past an unresolved issue and simply act as if it's resolved, declining attendance, difficulty scheduling an extra meeting, difficulty finding a volunteer in the group to take on extra duty, and so on. Both the chair and the facilitator should be on the lookout for these warning signs and be prepared to tackle them head-on. The group has come too far, and has too much invested, to drop the ball at this point.

Sometimes all that's needed is a review of progress to date ("think of where we were when we started!"), or a clear statement of exactly what remains to be done (people generally have more difficulty facing an unknown burden than a known one). It may be that such a statement needs to be made toward the end of the deciding phase ("There is still work to be done—involving steps A, B, and C—and the members of this group are the only ones who can finish it.").

The second pitfall to guard against is **defensiveness**—specifically, excessive sensitivity to criticism of the group's work. As we will see in subsequent sections of this chapter, the implementation phase is when the product of the CBA process has to be taken out into the world and subjected to tough scrutiny. When you solicit opinions from people who haven't been involved, what you get back in response is not always fun to hear. In fact, it can be demoralizing or infuriating. This can be particularly true for members of the group who haven't before been involved in politics or other kinds of public processes.

Hearing your proposed agreement criticized is a lot like listening to someone find fault with one of your children. Negotiators can get prickly and defensive when the fruits of their hard work are criticized. Again, defensiveness is something for the chair, the facilitator, or other leaders of the process to be on guard against. It's good to be proud of your work and to be invested in it. (In fact, as we'll make clear below, we're going to *insist* that you be invested in your work in the sense of committing to the final agreement.) But a balance needs to be struck. It's not good to be so defensive that you can't hear what people are saying, as they respond to your proposed agreement.

The check-off

Check-off, or ratification, is one of the most important elements of the larger CBA process. This is when the members of the group take their work back to their respective constituencies to "check off" with each of them. If those constituencies choose to ratify the agreement, then the group obviously has come up with a workable solution. If those constituencies don't ratify, the group has come up short.

How could the group come up short? It's not hard to imagine a credible scenario. Suppose that the people at the table have been working long and hard on a particularly difficult question. Given all the time and energy they've put in, they don't want to wind up with nothing. In an effort to salvage an agreement, the members of the negotiating group begin to pull away from the positions of the people they represent and drift toward some sort of middle ground. The danger is that in so doing, they cease to represent the interests of their respective groups.

What's needed, therefore, is a process by which each of the negotiators takes a copy of the proposed agreement back to his or her constituency to seek the approval of that group. In many cases, such constituencies are very different from each other. That argues for a ratification process that may be very different from constituency to constituency. Inconsistency is perfectly OK, as long as the various methods of checking off are understood and approved in advance by all parties. Stated a little differently, **each person needs to be accountable to every other person around the table for the method(s) they intend to use to canvass their constituents**.

Of course, the canvassers have to deliver on these promises. They actually have to do the work they've promised and bring back any significant concerns that their discussions with their respective constituents may have identified.

In earlier chapters, we've talked about the need to "go slow to go fast." This is an example. It's sometimes tempting to rush through the check-off phase. Think of the two psychological issues raised above:

burn-out, and defensiveness. Burn-out might lead a negotiator to say, "Oh, what the heck. I talked to Sally and John at the coffee shop, and Bob at church, and Marlee at the supermarket, and nobody had any strong feelings about the proposed agreement; enough's enough!" Defensiveness might cause a negotiator to say, "Well, two of the first three people I talked to took cheap shots at our proposal, thereby demonstrating their complete ignorance of the complex issues on the table; enough's enough!"

It's risky to declare victory based on inadequate evidence or when you're caught up in emotions. Each negotiator has to take the pulse of his constituents dispassionately and figure out how much support the emerging agreement can command. He has to be able to say honestly to the others at the table that his group will work to make implementation of the agreement succeed, and as a result, the agreement will be nearly self-enforcing. Or, he has to state candidly what will have to change to get that particular constituency on board. Then, the group will have to decide how to handle such requests.

Depending on your particular circumstances, there may be other steps your group can take to reinforce the check-off process. Basically, your goal is to get potential objections to the agreement on the table so you can figure out a way to deal with them. What are the chances that there are other interested parties sitting out there whom you've decided aren't interested but actually are, or whom you don't even know?

Sometimes putting the draft agreement in the local newspaper can help (when a CBA in the public arena is involved), assuming your local paper will agree to assist in this way. (Many won't.) Sometimes a website or a mass mailing (paper or e-mail) can serve a similar purpose. If you go this route, of course, you will want to be sensible about distribution: who is unlikely to be reached by your communication? Certain newspapers tend to reach only certain kinds of people; e-mail tends to reach younger and more affluent populations. If we are talking about a CBA inside an organization, it should be much easier to reach all the relevant constituents.

You will also want to be careful about sequencing the distribution of your news. As a general rule, the known constituencies should hear first about the proposed solution from their own representatives rather than coming across the plan in the local paper, or on a website, or via e-mail.

Committing to the final agreement

The check-off process may simply serve to ratify the existing proposal. Or, it may necessitate changes, which may, in turn, necessitate another round of ratification.

In either case, the next step is to commit to the final agreement. What's needed here is a **personal commitment on the part of each group member**. We need to stress that the participants are not formally committing their respective constituencies to the agreement. In most cases, they don't have the authority to do that, even if they have been formally designated as their constituency's representative at the table. The representative of an ad hoc neighborhood group, for example, probably can't commit the members of that group to a particular agreement and couldn't enforce such a commitment if she tried. (As noted earlier, a *self*-enforcing mechanism is the goal.) Instead, the commitment step is intended to accomplish two things: (1) to get all the negotiators to confirm that they have, indeed, done what they promised to do, in terms of canvassing their constituencies and bringing back relevant issues to the table, and (2) to get each representative to confirm, in writing, that she will stand up publicly and support the agreement.

In drafting this "memo of commitment," it is very important to strike the right tone. On the one hand, your group most likely adopted a consensus-building approach in part because it wanted to avoid the rigidity, formality, and legalism of Robert's Rules. That decision argues for informality and argues *against* throwing a lot of legalese on the table at the eleventh hour. On the other hand, committing to an agreement is serious business. Whatever form the memo takes, it should reflect that seriousness.

Checking off in Blaine

It's time to revisit our negotiators on the Blaine Bicentennial Committee and see how their proposal is faring during implementation.

You will recall that the members of the BCC had gone back to their respective constituencies, gotten feedback, and made changes in the plan. At the table, and with facilitator Connie's help, the group hammered out a revised version, which the group ultimately endorsed unanimously.

In real life, that might have been the end of the process. But let's imagine, for the sake of illustration, that Connie informed the group that another, more formal round of checking off and committing was needed. Imagine, also, that she asked each member of the group to put in writing the steps he or she planned to take to check off with their constituency. The conversation might sound something like this:

CONNIE: Let's go around the table and have each of you read your statement of what you plan to do to get buy-in out there in the world. Then, if you'll pass that statement around the table to Molly, she can compile them into a single document, which I'm going to ask all of you to initial. Bill, let's give the chairman the honor of going first.

BILL: Well, really, I think I've already done most of what's needed. But here's what I wrote down: "I will sit down with the mayor and get him to initial the latest version of the draft agreement, which includes him selling the plan to whichever other pols and bigwigs he thinks are important. Meanwhile, I will get our half-dozen or so private donors, including my own company, to confirm in writing that they plan to underwrite specific parts of the celebration."

CONNIE: Great. But maybe since this is a public document, Bill, I think I'll ask Molly to change "pols and bigwigs" to "other political leaders."

BILL: [*laughs*] Fine. I'll make the change myself. The mayor will know what I *really* meant.

VINCE: I guess I'm next, if we're going clockwise around the table. I wrote, "I will ask for a formal vote of the Historical Commission to endorse the plan." Not very complicated.

CONNIE: Maybe not complicated but very important. Ralph?

RALPH: OK. "First, I will confirm with the Theatrical Guild that they are willing to give us a one-time, non-precedent-setting exemption from their work rules, permitting us to put union and nonunion actors on stage together. With that answer in hand, I will bring together the relevant faculty and administrators from our schools, tell them exactly what we need them to do, and make sure they're OK with that." Except for the union, I really don't anticipate any difficulties.

CONNIE: Sally?

SALLY: Well, my situation is a little different. I can't really call together my board of directors or my commission and ask for any kind of vote. I'm not dealing with an organized group. I'm just hearing from a couple of loosely organized groups of African Americans, as well as my volunteer networks.

CONNIE: We understand that you have to take a different approach from the others at the table. What did you write?

SALLY: "I will get back in touch with each person who contacted me, and ask them to host a meeting of individuals who may be interested in the bicentennial. In addition, I will put notices in the bulletins of the local African American churches, inviting people to get in touch with me about the bicentennial plans."

VINCE: Sounds a little squishy, I have to say. What happens the day after you finish this round of meetings and some new group pops up and starts making demands on us?

SALLY: Well, like I already said, Vince, you've got it easy. You just call together the same six old cronies you've been meeting with for—what? twenty years?—take a vote, and call it a night. No heavy lifting over at the Historical Commission.

VINCE: Maybe the difference is, I've already *done* my homework.

SALLY: So you're suggesting I haven't?

CONNIE: Come on, guys; we're all doing our homework. Let me point out that the problem Vince and Sally are talking about is very common in efforts like this. We're all trying to accomplish the same thing—to get people on board with the agreement—but we're all talking to different people, so we have to proceed in different ways.

MOLLY: May I make a suggestion?

CONNIE: Of course.

MOLLY: Well, it seemed to work pretty well when Vince took me along with him to talk with the Historical Commission. Maybe Sally could take me to some or all of her meetings and let me talk up the website as a community resource, something people can get involved in. You know, accentuate the positive. Of course, only if she thinks that's a good idea.

SALLY: Sounds fine to me. You might be wasting your time, though, if people are all fired up about where they're going to be marching in the parade.

MOLLY: That's all right. As I see it, I don't have any constituencies of my own to look after. All I could think up to write down was, "I will go back to my programmers and designers and get a solid commitment of donated time from them in the weeks leading up to the June launch. I will also make myself available to explain the website to anyone who wants to hear more about it."

I didn't write this part up, because I wasn't sure what the group would think about it. I have a standing offer from the host of a local cable show to go on her show and talk about the state of the high-tech world. It occurred to me that I could take her up on that offer and talk up the website. Is that OK with the rest of you?

BILL: Makes good sense to me. You'd have to put it in the context of the bigger effort, though, showing how all this stuff ties together.

VINCE: Seems to me that if we're going that route, we ought to try to get the *Blaine Times* to write up what we're planning and maybe even run the proposal verbatim.

CONNIE: Logically, Bill, that job would fall to you as the chair. How strong are your ties to the editor?

BILL: Well, my company certainly is one of his biggest advertisers, and he and I play golf together now and then. I think I could get that ball rolling downhill.

CONNIE: Anybody have a problem with the TV and newspaper plans? No? Then I'll ask Molly to add "TV contact" to her own assignment and "newspaper contact" to Bill's. Have you got the statements compiled yet, Molly?

MOLLY: Just finishing now. Let me add the TV and newspaper jobs. There. Done.

CONNIE: Now, Molly, if you could initial it at the bottom and pass it on ... thanks. ... Again, the point of this exercise is to get everybody at the table on the same page about who's doing what in terms of getting people out in the world to sign on to this proposal.

At our next meeting, which I'd like to ask Bill to schedule for a week from tonight, we're going to deal with whatever issues come up as a result of these conversations. Then, I'm going to ask you all to sign the agreement itself.

VINCE: Connie, I need to say something at this point.

CONNIE: Fire away, Vince.

VINCE: I have to say that I thought we had wrapped this all up at our *last* meeting. Now you're talking about another meeting and maybe more meetings after that. Frankly, I'm getting a little tired of all these meetings.

SALLY: Hear, hear.

VINCE: I didn't sign on for life with this thing. So my question is, when is it going to end?

CONNIE: I can understand your frustration, Vince, and I think I heard Sally agreeing with you, and I bet some of the rest of you feel the same way. Last time, we agreed to a plan that talked about the end game, including ways to monitor the agreement. Now here we are, seemingly opening everything up again.

VINCE: Exactly.

CONNIE: Well, the real answer to your question is, "probably sometime soon." The fact that you all *have* been doing your homework, right along, gives me confidence that we won't encounter any real difficulties in this check-off phase.

We're going to have to come up with a to-do list at our next meeting and assign those tasks to specific people, either in this group or outside the group. When those tasks are completed, or least well underway, I think we can call the process done.

Linking the informal to the formal

By the time you have canvassed constituents, dealt with any issues that have arisen as a result of the check-off process, and committed (as individuals) to the agreement, you are well on the way toward implementation. The remaining few steps, however, also need careful attention.

The first of these is making the link between the informal and the formal. What do we mean by this? Simply, there are likely to be a number of existing processes—political, legal, regulatory, and so on—with which this agreement needs to be "consistent." There may also be contingent side agreements and parallel commitments that have to be called upon and honored.

For example, we've stressed that most consensus-building efforts are advisory. This means that at some point, the group's advice has to be taken to the relevant body or bodies for review and action. If the group has been wrestling with a proposed rezoning of a particular parcel of land, and if the local zoning board is the body that ultimately makes land-use decisions, then the group's proposal has to be handed off to that board.

Similarly, it may be that the budget for a proposed agreement is contingent upon some other group reaching agreement. Maybe a vote of the city council is needed to make these funds available. It may be that private organizations have made commitments to do certain things in support of the agreement, in the event that it is ratified. Now is the time to set those wheels in motion.

In many situations, this involves thinking through a lot of small details, and asking and answering all the questions relating to those details. If the agreement calls for a parade, for example, and if the parade requires a permit, who's going to apply for that permit? Who's going to make sure that the town's rules regarding parades are followed? If the Chamber of Commerce has pledged $500 in support of the parade, who's going to follow up with that group, get the check cut, take it to city hall, and make sure that the funds are deposited in the right account?

Does that account exist yet? If not, who can set it up? Who is authorized to disburse funds from that account? Are there any restrictions on funds deposited in that kind of account?

Since all of these details pertain to the implementation of an agreement that has already been approved, they shouldn't stir up undue controversy. (The "what" has already been agreed to; this is the "how.") Although the details described most likely have been included in the agreement—for example, the commitment to deliver the group's recommendation to the zoning board—these lower-level housekeeping details may not need to be included as part of the formal agreement. By the same token, they should be **written down**, with responsibilities for specific tasks assigned to specific groups or individuals. The members of the consensus-building group may want to initial this document, to indicate that they've seen it and signed off on it.

Each implementation plan is unique. Sometimes the consensus-building group doesn't need to take responsibility for performing any of these tasks itself. (The "formal" body, such as the zoning board, takes responsibility.) In other cases, its members have to involve themselves in all the specific tasks of implementation. Finally, this is another juncture when the leaders of the consensus-building effort may need to keep a watchful eye for signs of burn-out. If certain individuals have had enough, it makes no sense to load them down with implementation-related tasks.

These same considerations apply when CBA is being used in a purely private context. A company task force that has worked for many months to generate a proposed change in policy would not want to ignore the details of how its recommendations will be implemented. Indeed, it's hard to imagine that any group of people who have invested time and energy in a problem-solving process would ignore the final steps required to put their suggestions into action. While Robert's Rules require nothing more than an up-or-down vote to reach the finish line, CBA demands attention to everything that could possibly go wrong as well as clarity about who will do what to make sure the desired results are achieved.

Committing and "translating" in Blaine

A week has gone by. The BCC convenes once again, and each member of the group reports on his or her meetings. As expected, Sally has had the most difficult time getting the plan ratified since her constituency is the most diffused. She wound up having a series of small meetings in people's living rooms as well as one larger meeting in a church fellowship hall. Although a few people made comments about the unofficial marchers being located at the back of the parade ("Back to the back of the bus!" one person yelled out), most people seemed satisfied with the overall plan. Molly attended all the meetings and spoke at several of them. A few people took Molly's business card, expressing an interest in helping to develop content about Blaine's African American heritage. Several people volunteered to contribute pictures from family photograph albums.

Vince secured a unanimous vote from the Historical Commission. (The commission was very interested to learn—from Molly, via Vince—that new historical material, including photographs, might be forthcoming from the African American community.) Bill got the mayor's OK and signature on a copy of the proposal, along with his assurances that he would "sell" the package to the other politicians who had expressed an interest in participating on Saturday morning. Bill also rounded up written commitments from the private donors and managed to get interviewed by the *Blaine Times*. The editor declined to print the text of the full agreement, citing space constraints, but the gist of the proposal came through in the published interview. So far, the article had not generated any public response, although it had just come out. (The editor also wrote a favorable if somewhat inaccurate editorial, commenting on the consensus-building process that led up to the proposal.) Similarly, Molly's TV appearance had been taped and aired once, and it was likely to be aired a few more times in the coming weeks, and no one had raised any objections to the plan she described.

Ralph hammered out an agreement with the Theatrical Guild regarding the appearance of union actors with nonunion actors. Tonight, he has brought along to the meeting a copy of the agreement, which simply states that this is a one-time exception to the rules and is not precedent-setting, and as he lays it on the table, he makes an interesting observation:

RALPH: The thing I had to admit to them was that I had no idea who was going to sign it for *our* side. And frankly, I was damn lucky that they agreed to sign first. My own unions always insist on *us* signing first.

CONNIE: That raises the issue of turning things over to the appropriate authorities, which we were going to cover tonight, anyway.

Let's back up a step. First of all, it sounds like you all did a great job explaining and selling the agreement to your constituencies. It sounds like we can stick with the agreement in its current form. It also sounds like Bill and Molly have started to get the word out to the broader public. It's possible that this will generate some new conversations, but we'll have to wait and see.

VINCE: So we could have skipped that whole step, right, Connie? And saved a week, and maybe cut out a meeting?

CONNIE: Well, everybody is entitled to an opinion about that, Vince.

BILL: What's *your* opinion, Connie?

CONNIE: My opinion? I'm glad we have Vince's commission on record as being in support of the plan. I'm glad the mayor initialed it, and I'm glad that Ralph used his negotiating skills so successfully with the actors' union. I think it's a good thing that Sally and Molly worked hard to get the word out to the African American community, which in my view often gets left out of these discussions, especially in the early stages. It's always a good idea to firm up financial commitments.

So all in all, I think it was time well spent.

BILL: A good answer. What else is on the agenda tonight, Connie? Turning things over to other people?

CONNIE: That's part of it. The other part is getting you all to sign the agreement. You've already voted to approve the agreement in its present form. I'm passing around a copy for each of you to review. Tonight, I'm going to ask you all to sign all six copies—one for each of us—which will represent your personal commitment to make this plan work. Let me stress that you're only signing as *individuals*. In other words, Vince isn't committing the Historical Commission and Ralph isn't committing the school system. It's important to have all of us committed in writing to making this plan succeed.

BILL: Has this document we're looking at changed from last time? Based on a quick scan, all that seems to be new is this Exhibit B at the end, "Implementation assignments," with a reference to "Exhibit B" in the text. There's space for our signatures, of course.

CONNIE: Right. Those are the only changes, along with renaming the budget worksheet "Exhibit A."

Let me say a word about Exhibit B. This is simply my first cut at the list of things that have to get done in order to push the agreement along and get other people to take responsibility. It's housekeeping, in a sense, but it's also more than that. It's how we transform our work from the report of an advisory group into a real commitment on the part of people and groups in the town.

Since I'm going to ask you to sign this, too, let's take some time to read it and amend it as necessary.

The group reviews Connie's proposed list and makes a few additions. The result is as shown in the table on the following page.

When these discussions are completed, Connie retrieves all six copies, signs each on the line above her name, and passes them along to Bill, on her right. The six copies pass from hand to hand with much rustling of paper and banter. When they all arrive back at Connie's seat, she hands one out to each of the other five people and keeps one for herself.

"Congratulations," she says. "We are almost there."

Designing monitoring mechanisms

As part of the implementation process, consensus-building groups need to pay close attention to the task of **monitoring**. This can be considered in two parts: (1) monitoring to ensure that the individuals and groups involved are honoring their commitments, and (2) monitoring to ensure that the world hasn't changed in some way that calls for a change in the agreement.

EXHIBIT B "IMPLEMENTATION ASSIGNMENTS"

Event/Task	Who?	Who nudges?
Administrative		
Present approved plan to mayor	Bill	
Set up dedicated checking account	Town treasurer	Bill
Get checks from donors	Bill	
Take checks to treasurer	Bill	
Dramatic presentation		
Hire professional actors	Ralph (and school staff)	
Write script, begin set design, etc.	School staff and actors	Ralph
Reserve auditorium; hire custodians	Ralph (and school staff)	
Write program/memento	Historical Commission (HC)	Vince
Sync up Fri night/Sat morning content	HC/Mayor's office	Vince and Sally
Parade		
Secure permit	Bill	
Design/approve floats	DPW/Mayor's office	Bill
Arrange for police overtime	Mayor's office	Bill
Hire/supervise clean-up crew	DPW/Mayor's office	Bill
Speeches/ceremony		
AV system rental	Mayor's office	Bill
Stage/bunting/banners	Mayor's office	Bill
Prepare time capsule contents	Schools and HC	Ralph, Vince
Prep time capsule site	DPW/Mayor's office	Bill
Field day/crafts fair		
Contact arts/crafts groups	Sally	
Arrange for police overtime	Mayor's office	Bill
Rent portable toilets	Park Department	Sally
Rent/buy sports equipment	Park Department	Sally
"Hire" baseball team	Mayor's office	Bill
Hire/supervise clean-up crew	DPW/Mayor's office	Bill
Arrange for food/beverages	Park Department	Sally
Fireworks		
Buy/prep pyrotechnics	Mayor's office	Bill
Prepare site	Mayor's office	Bill
Website		
Coordinate with HC	Molly/Vince	
Arrange for photo scans	Molly	
Supervise programming	Molly	
Supervise community outreach	Molly	
Publicity		
Cultivate newspaper	Bill	
Cultivate WBLA radio	Bill	
Cultivate cable TV	Molly	

The first of these two types of monitoring should be reasonably easy to handle. (In fact, in some cases, it's not even necessary to spell out this "policing" function.) Will the consensus-building group meet every six months for the next three years to make sure that the townwide technology master plan is being implemented in accordance with the agreement, or, will the town administrator simply make an annual report to town meeting? If the group's sense is that a formal monitoring mechanism is needed to help enforce commitments—even though, as we want to keep stressing, the agreement is intended to be *nearly self-enforcing*—this mechanism should be defined clearly and written into the agreement. If someone isn't keeping her promise, what is the mechanism for reconvening and reopening the discussion?

The second kind of monitoring mechanism tends to be trickier. Most agreements that grow out of consensus-building efforts pertain to corners of the world that are subject to change. Implementing the town-wide technology master plan, for example, depends on the sale of bonds; but this assumes that interest rates won't go through the roof and the town's bond rating will hold up. Well, what happens in the event that one of these assumptions proves wrong? Or what if a dazzling new technology appears on the scene in Year Two, which calls for a rethinking of the master plan? What if the state board of education issues an unfunded mandate calling for new and expensive technologies in the schools?

Again, the consensus-building group probably needs to reach an understanding **up front** about who's going to get together and what they're going to do, if unforeseen circumstances change the playing field. This understanding probably needs to be included in the final version of the agreement. Note the word "probably." If it's clear that the agreement can be turned over to a governing body once and for all, and if that body can (and should) handle future eventualities, it may not be necessary to write the obvious in the agreement. Otherwise, again, the procedure for reconvening and reopening needs to be spelled out clearly in the agreement.

Different groups react differently to the prospect of monitoring and reconvening mechanisms. Once again, the issue of burn-out raises its head. ("What??? You're saying this is a *three-year* commitment??!! You're saying we may get called back together???!!") Obviously, this argues for making the monitoring burden a manageable task—one that is assigned to willing individuals and groups.

In some cases, individuals may be wary about adding a mechanism for changing the hard-won agreement, fearing that somebody in the future may abuse that opportunity. If and when those concerns arise, it's worth reminding those wary individuals that the consensus-building group brought itself together in the first place to reach the **best possible agreement**, rather than a bad compromise or a zero-sum, Robert's Rules-type outcome. If circumstances change enough so that there's a new **best agreement possible**, then, in the spirit of the original convening of the group, there should be a mechanism to get to that new possibility.

In our experience, however, most groups quickly grasp the importance of a monitoring mechanism, and in fact, insist on it being included in the final version of any agreement. Similarly, it may be desirable to include what is often called a "dispute resolution clause" in the agreement. This spells out how differences of opinion regarding who has or has not lived up to their commitments should be handled. It may be that the parties agree to designate the chair or the facilitator as the point of contact if one party feels that another member of the group has not done what she promised. Most dispute resolution clauses make it clear that no one can unilaterally disavow his commitments because he *thinks* that someone else has failed to meet their obligations. This avoids the prospect of a whole agreement falling apart when one person mistakenly assumes that another has not lived up to her commitments. Instead, a period of time is often specified during which the designated point of contact can undertake an investigation, reconvene the group, and report back what they found so the group can decide together what they want to do.

Evaluating, capturing, and communicating

We include this last step in the "recommended but optional" category. Assume that you're at the end of a long and ultimately productive CBA. It goes without saying that you've learned a lot as a group. You've learned things that another group coming along behind you should definitely keep in mind as they begin their own consensus-building effort—things they should try to do, and things they should try *not* to do.

We strongly recommended that your group **evaluate** what it has gone through, while memories are still fresh, **capture** the relevant lessons, and find appropriate ways to **communicate** what has been learned.

Presumably, this "captured wisdom" should be contained in a companion document to the main agreement. It might be prepared around the same time as the main agreement or, with support from the group, shortly thereafter. Just like the main agreement, this document should not be seen as an exercise in score-keeping: who was right about what and who was wrong. It should avoid attributing positions or actions (good or bad) to individuals and instead focus on recommendations and prescriptions.

Your goal, in evaluating, capturing, and communicating, is not to pat yourselves on the back. Rather, it is to help your institution, organization, or community learn how to be more successful at doing these things in the future. Maybe no one will ever thank you for making this extra effort, but maybe they will.

When is it "over"?

Implementation is the last step in consensus building. We are often asked to define when a CBA can be considered "over." The simplest answer is, "It's over when the last person named does the last task described."

Or, using the language of this chapter, consensus building ends when the agreement is ratified by the affected constituencies and endorsed by the participants, when appropriate monitoring and reconvening mechanisms are in place, and when formal responsibility for the agreement has been handed over to the responsible parties.

Obviously, the monitoring function extends beyond this point; in the event that the group needs to reconvene, a new round of work obviously must begin. For all practical purposes, though, successful implementation of an agreement signals the end of the consensus-building group's obligations. Our final recommendation, growing out of the implementation phase is this: the group should make a point of celebrating a job well done.

In our next and final chapter, we step back from the mechanics of CBA and describe a range of barriers to such efforts. We describe the kinds of challenges that are often raised to consensus building and suggest ways they can be overcome.

Key Terms and Concepts Explained in Chapter 7
(For further clarification, see Part 2:
The Five Essential Steps in the
Consensus Building Approach, step 5, page 185)

Nearly self-enforcing agreements
Threats to implementation
Burn-out
Defensiveness
Checking back with constituents
Personal commitments to implement the agreement
Linking the informal and the formal
Designing monitoring mechanisms
Adding dispute resolution clauses

8

⟿

Overcoming the Barriers to CBA

Consensus building can get you to far better solutions than Robert's Rules. CBA is often the best way to generate an agreement that is fairer, more efficient, wiser, and more stable than would otherwise be possible.

That begs an obvious question: if CBA is such a superior approach, why isn't the whole world doing it?

There are several reasons:

- **General Robert had a serious head start.** *Robert's Rules* became widely available in the late nineteenth century. Consensus building (as we practice it today) is only a few decades old.
- **Robert's Rules are the "law."** This is an outgrowth of the previous point. As noted in chapter 1, a wide range of institutions, public and private, have articles of incorporation or bylaws that specifically call for the use of Robert's Rules. Our strong sense is that for many of these groups, parliamentary procedure is no longer the most appropriate approach, if it ever was. Think about it: Robert's Rules and the telegraph were invented at the same time. When a better alternative (the telephone) became available, the telegraph slowly withered away. We assume the same

will happen with Robert's Rules, but inertia is a powerful force in the public arena.

- **There are perceptual barriers to consensus building.** People favor the tried-and-true, especially when they are under pressure. Many groups assume that CBA is difficult, costly, too time-consuming, or of uncertain efficacy. They worry about undermining the "democratic process," which they support in principle. In this chapter, we will argue that such concerns are misplaced.

- **There are external barriers to consensus building.** Based on our real-world experience, we can point to three external barriers to effective consensus building. One is that an individual determined to disrupt the process can, indeed, cause serious trouble. The second is that the media tend to take a neutral-to-negative stand, vis-à-vis CBA. The third is that people worry about liability or otherwise running afoul of the law. Later in this chapter, we will suggest ways in which these barriers can be overcome. First, let's look at the perceptual barriers.

Overcoming the perceptual barriers

There is substantial evidence to suggest that CBA produces agreements that save time and money, increase the level of satisfaction of all parties, and are more likely to be implemented successfully. In some cases, though, there are obstacles to consensus building generated by people who anticipate problems. We call these "perceptual barriers" because they loom large in the minds of the beholders. What are they, specifically?

A fear of the unknown.   The first perceptual barrier is fear of change. Apparently because of the way human beings are "hard-wired," the power of the status quo is extraordinary. Doing things a new way involves uncertainty and risk (or at least the *prospect* of risk). Most people favor the known over the unknown. Especially when they are under pressure, they favor the tried-and-true over the unproven. This often takes the form of a question: *We've always settled our differences in a certain way; why should we change?*

The answer that we offer is, *If everything is going fine now, then you probably shouldn't change.* If your existing approach to identifying and resolving complicated problems is working, great. But, if you're spending more time, energy, and money than you'd like in order to arrive at outcomes that in the end lead some people to walk away angry—and determined to undo what you've done—then perhaps it's time to try something different.

A fear of failure.   A second and related perceptual barrier is that people are concerned that their lack of familiarity with CBA will lead to failure.

That's why we have written this book. We've tried to capture both the nuts-and-bolts procedures as well as the spirit of consensus building, and to illustrate them via regular visits to our fictional friends on the Blaine Bicentennial Committee. (More on them shortly.) We believe that if you follow these procedures and do business in the spirit described in the previous chapters, you will succeed.

But this little book isn't your only resource. There is a huge array of resources available to you, probably in or near your hometown and certainly within striking distance. Consensus-building support is provided by professionals who practice nationally and internationally. (Every state in America has practitioners, often to be found in the phone book under "mediation" or something similar.) Associated professions, such as the law, are increasingly aware of these alternatives. The Web provides easy access to skilled facilitators. A Google search of consensus building, or what is sometimes called "alternative dispute resolution," turns up literally hundreds of thousands of links—in fact, close to a million. With a little trial-and-error research, you can narrow this universe down to a manageable size.

So help is out there. In addition, consensus building is a very natural way to solve problems; far more natural, for example, than using Robert's Rules. Think of it this way: if you were inventing your own society from scratch, how would you want its members to handle their differences? Probably by getting together, identifying their respective interests, and looking for a solution that did the most good for the most people —without sacrificing anyone's most basic interests. It's intuitive. Once people get a feel for CBA, they *know* that it's the way to go.

A reluctance to embrace a process that may be slow, costly, etc.   A third perceptual barrier is that people think of consensus building as too slow, too cumbersome, or too costly. This brings us back to our definition of consensus, introduced in chapter 1. We are *not* advocating a process in which everybody talks until they are blue in the face, and in which unanimity is achieved through "trial by blather." Far from it! Instead, we are advocating a step-by-step approach in which people work hard to achieve what we call "overwhelming agreement." This can take time. Again, risking the wrath of our seventh-grade grammar teachers, you have to *go slow to go fast*.

We also ask, "Slow and costly in comparison to what?" In chapter 1, we described the problem-solving process governed by Robert's Rules and parliamentary procedure. These processes, too, take time. If they create an unhappy minority, moreover, the "solutions" they produce may not be durable. If a decision comes unstuck, and if that means the whole scenario has to be rerun—whether because an election injects new players, or a court intervenes to overturn some aspect of an agreement, or some other unexpected development crops up—then that's a different kind of "slow and costly."

Yes, hiring a facilitator costs something (if an outside facilitator is needed). Conducting joint fact-finding—most often in the context of a significant public dispute, like the North Atlantic fisheries dispute described in chapter 5—can be expensive.

But again, expensive compared to what? We sometimes use a phrase, the "cost of contentiousness," to make this point. Think of the enormous amounts of time, money, and energy spent on lawyers and litigation. (Increasingly, lawyers and judges are tending to agree that certain kinds of disputes shouldn't wind up in court.) On a more grassroots level, think of how much time and energy—and indirectly, financial resources—go into trying to influence a town meeting vote. People run for office, make secret deals behind the scenes, prepare presentations, swap votes, and so on. Then, if they don't like the outcome, they have to do it all again during the next election cycle. Or, to cite an increasingly popular gambit, they force a recall of the offending public official(s). Now, *that's* expensive, especially when you factor in the delays, uncertainties, and anxieties associated with such tactics.

A reluctance to undermine authority.   By invoking town meeting, we raise the last, and perhaps the most important, perceptual barrier to CBA. Some people worry that consensus building undermines the authority of those elected or appointed to perform certain tasks. When the Blaine town meeting authorized the mayor to organize a bicentennial celebration—so this reasoning goes—that body conferred responsibility on *him.* Shouldn't he do the job himself? Or, looked at from the other side, why should anybody else expect to be involved in a decision that is clearly the mayor's responsibility?

These are reasonable questions, but there are good answers. First, we contend that the mayor is not abdicating his responsibilities by seeking advice from a representative group of stakeholders. (Most likely, he gets advice all the time, although not usually through a process as transparent as consensus building.) In fact, he *should* get all the input he can to carry out his job effectively, and he should get as much as possible through CBA. Shouldn't he get advice through a public process, rather than a secret one?

Second, like it or not, the trajectory of the last century or so of politics in the United States has been toward a broader base of involvement. People want to express their views on issues that are important to them. Increasingly, they are unwilling to simply elect public officials and hope for the best. They expect to be consulted, and involved in, decisions that affect their lives. Consensus building is a way of shaping democratic involvement and making it more efficient.

As suggested above, the end product of every consensus-building effort is **advice**. Throughout the preceding chapters, we used the word "proposal" to describe the product of the Blaine Bicentennial Committee. In one sense, its plan was being proposed to the various constituencies that had a stake in the outcome. On a more fundamental level, though, the BCC was making a proposal—offering advice—to the mayor. He could choose to embrace or ignore it.

Think about it: here's a way for the mayor to know ahead of time the actions he can take that will get (almost) everybody to stand up and cheer. What elected or appointed official wouldn't want *that* kind of input?

Overcoming the external barriers

So much for the barriers to CBA that exist mainly in people's minds. Let's move on to some more substantial obstacles to successful consensus building and think about how these might be overcome as well. These include:

- Disruptive behavior by a participant in the process
- Media problems
- Legal complications

Disruptive behavior by a participant.   We've all been there: serving as part of a group of volunteers when one member refuses to play by the rules. It can be the book club, the church choir, the company softball team, or almost any other organization. When one person sets out to disrupt a group, it can be poisonous. This is particularly true in the context of CBA, which depends on collaboration and joint problem solving.

First, let's make a distinction between "argumentative" and "obstructionist." If you think about the positions that Vince (the Historical Commission's representative) took on the BCC, he was frequently argumentative, to the point where Connie sometimes had to step in and keep the group on track. Yet, Vince's argumentativeness mostly stayed within bounds and often served to move the dialog along. In many cases, in fact, a skilled facilitator can work with an argumentative participant and even use that person as a means of helping the group: "Vince makes an interesting point. Restating it slightly, I think Vince is reminding us that we have to worry about such-and-such."

An obstructionist, by contrast, isn't committed to making the process work and may even be committed to making it fail. Obstructionists come in three types, going from bad to worse:

1. Individuals who have little or no experience working in groups and act out their insecurities in unproductive ways.
2. Individuals who have made their way through life by being disruptive, and don't see any reason to alter their approach.
3. Individuals who think that their interests, or their constituency's interests, lie in sabotaging the effort.

It would be great, of course, if you could simply keep obstructionists out of the process. But in a convening effort, as described in chapter 3, you need to make sure that all key constituencies are represented. If key constituency A sends you an obstructionist, you probably need to find a way to make that work.

We can point to three important resources. The first is a good set of **ground rules**, also described in chapter 3. Each consensus-building process is unique and needs its own set of rules. Preparing such rules offers an opportunity for each group to discuss relevant behavioral norms and internalize them. At the beginning of the CBA, therefore, the members of the group need to define and adopt a set of behaviors, and to hold each other to them. It's generally a good idea to write down such rules and to get people to sign off on them. If someone refuses to sign a statement that accurately summarizes the ground rules that they've already agreed to, that's an early sign of trouble. If everyone signs, that means that the facilitator or chair is free to point to those rules and insist on conformance to them.

The second resource, of course, is a **skilled facilitator**. Through training and experience, facilitators learn to ride herd on tense proceedings. At the right moment, as suggested above, they cite the ground rules. Or, they take on obstructionists directly, keeping the other participants out of harm's way. A trained facilitator knows when to stop the meeting and take an offending individual aside for a private conference. Or she might halt the process temporarily and look for ways to restructure negotiations so that the obstructionist can be heard, but isn't necessarily seated at the table, perhaps through some informal type of "shuttle diplomacy."

Skilled facilitators understand what motivates obstructionists, and they use that understanding to limit the damage. Some obstructionists "play to the grandstand," in an effort to prove to their constituents that they are being "tough at the table." An able facilitator makes sure that such behavior is not rewarded. The communications that go out from the group, for example, never attribute specific positions to individuals. Gradually, the obstructionist realizes (or should realize) that her actions aren't achieving the outcomes she desires.

A third resource is **training**. People sometimes roll their eyes when they think about committing even more time to an already time-consuming process. We would make two observations in response. First, training can be as simple as an hour or two of instruction before the first formal meeting of the group. (In other words, it doesn't have to involve a major time commitment.) Second, certain participants—especially those who have had little experience working in groups—may decide that it's in their best interest to get better at what they're about to do, so that they can represent their constituencies more effectively.

Sometimes, obstructionists act in the ways that they do out of insecurity. Training may reduce that insecurity and give them another way to advance their interests. Training can come at almost any point in the process, although it's generally better to cast training in terms of up-front skill-building rather than as mid-course fire-fighting.

Media problems.   Our second external barrier to effective consensus building is poor communication. This sometimes grows out of the bad habits of people at the table, but it more often grows out of difficulties created by the media.

On the first point: sometimes people who come to a consensus-building effort know only traditional, zero-sum, Robert's Rules bargaining. They are accustomed to using the press to advance their own negotiating stance—to amplify their particular concerns—at the expense of others. Again, the best tool for responding to this problem is a good set of ground rules that clearly state who can say what to the press. In general, the group designates one person (usually the chair or facilitator) to speak for the group. Beyond that, individuals are usually encouraged to speak for themselves but are prohibited from speaking for anybody else or from characterizing anyone else's views.

As a rule, posturing in the press disappears when individuals see progress at the table. Gradually, those involved come to understand that there's more to be gained at the table than on the front page of the paper. Again, a skilled facilitator can usually ensure that this understanding evolves.

The second communications challenge, which we'll politely summarize as "bad habits on the part of the media," is considerably more complicated and may call for a coordinated set of responses.

In many local disputes, the single most important medium is the local newspaper. (Metropolitan media outlets usually don't deign to cover local dustups; local radio stations have small audiences; community cable stations don't have the talent or resources to move quickly; and the Web is still too diffuse a medium to exert much local impact.) Most local newspapers see themselves as simply holding a mirror up to events. Sometimes, if they are honest, they will admit that they put a dramatic spin on stories to attract eyeballs and sell papers. Only rarely do they say that they have an obligation to educate the public or to shape public opinion (except in the limited context of editorials).

In recent years, the so-called public journalism movement has sought to expand the media's educational role in public debates. CBA would benefit greatly from a continued trend in this direction and away from the tradition of local papers fanning the flames of contentiousness. Of course, consensus builders can't sit around and wait for an ideal world to take shape. Here are a number of concrete steps that consensus builders can take to increase the odds of the media being helpful.

First, at the outset of the process, somebody—the convener, the chair, or the facilitator—needs to sit down with the media and alert them to the fact that *things are going to be done differently*, this time out. Ideally, such a conversation should be held with the owners of relevant media outlets, rather than the news directors or assignment editors. The premise behind such a discussion should be that the owners are interested parties, as business interests in the community, and therefore have a vested interest in having the consensus-building effort succeed. In our experience, owners (who tend to oversee editorials) often respond well to this approach.

Second, somebody in the group—whether the convener, the chair, or the facilitator—has to produce timely meeting summaries on a regular basis and get them to the media so that they have an accurate portrayal of the points of agreement reached at each step in the process. Somebody also has to be the central point of contact for the media, so that one voice can present a balanced version of what's going on at the negotiating sessions.

Is that enough? Absolutely not. In most cases, when you provide summaries to a newspaper, they will say that that they intend to produce their *own* summaries. Then they don't do it. The problem arises when reporters attend specific CBA sessions, and there's no drama. No one is shouting at anyone else or showboating for the cameras. There are no sound bites. So, the reporter finds little to write about and eventually stops attending.

You need to take additional steps to get the word out. For example, you need to generate your own mailing lists (e-mail and paper), develop and maintain a website, conduct periodic briefing sessions for appropriate audiences, make reports to boards or elected bodies as appropriate, and so on. Remember that in a situation like the one we followed in Blaine, **you can't communicate enough**. If the local newspaper declines to write articles or editorials, consider buying space in that paper or even paying for an insert to put a copy of the nearly completed agreement in the hands of every household in town. (It pains us to recommend this, but sometimes it turns out to be necessary.) Meanwhile, don't hesitate to point out to the owners of the paper or TV station that unless they accept some responsibility for educating the public, they will continue to undermine their own circulation and ratings because people will be driven to nontraditional media outlets, like the Web, for information.

Legal complications. This is the last of our three external barriers to consensus building. What happens when there is a legal process already underway that in some way intersects with the consensus-building process? More generally, what laws pertain to CBA? Do participants risk any kind of liability?

As for the first question—the circumstance of a consensus-building process running in tandem with a legal proceeding—we should cite a paragraph from one of our earlier works, *The Consensus Building Handbook*:

> If a consensus-building effort is meant to resolve issues that are simultaneously the subject of litigation, the participants in the informal consensus-building dialogue should be apprised by counsel of their legal rights, and the impact that informal consensus-building conversations might have on the legal proceedings and vice versa. They should also approach the judge or adjudication body to talk about the best way of coordinating the two processes.

Can you run two processes in parallel? Yes, although you must take steps to make it clear to everyone what's going on. The basic concept is that when people are litigating in civil cases, they're always free to try to try to settle out of court. (Criminal cases, obviously, are a different matter.) No matter how ugly or heated a dispute, there's no theoretical reason why the parties can't settle, drop the litigation, and go home. In many instances, in fact, judges strongly encourage them to do so.

Consensus building can and should be seen, and used, as a way to expand settlement options. Be aware, though, that there are ways in which things that are said in a CBA process can be demanded subsequently in court. Although facilitators usually can't be compelled to reveal confidential proceedings, individual participants might be called to testify as to who said what. Again, **good ground rules are important.** As implied above, the lawyers for all parties should be advising their respective clients as to what formal rules may apply to informal deliberations.

The second issue is **liability.** Can you be sued for slander as a result of something you say at a public negotiating session? The short answer is no. The American justice system, focused as it is on free speech as an underpinning of democracy, makes it extremely difficult to win a slander or a libel judgment. (Slander is spoken; libel is written.) To be held liable for slander, it needs to be shown that (1) you said something wrong, (2) you knew it was wrong, (3) you went ahead recklessly and repeated a falsehood in a willful effort to damage someone's reputation, and (4) some kind of real damage resulted.

Obviously, this is not what CBA is about. There's a first time for everything, of course, but to our knowledge, there has never been a successful slander or libel judgment brought against a participant in a consensus-building effort. Again, an effective set of ground rules (like, "disagree without being disagreeable") works against this kind of problem.

So does the very nature of consensus building. We bring ourselves together, giving up our Tuesday nights for weeks on end to solve a pressing problem. This is hard and serious work. Group norms quickly come into play. As Huck Finn said to Tom Sawyer, "Throwin' mud ain't arguing, Tom." We want to focus on arguing—arguing to a constructive purpose!—and not on mudslinging.

Reaching consensus: closing thoughts

Perhaps you are left wondering what happened to the Blaine Bicentennial Committee. Did the Friday night performance come off? Did the distinction between "official" and "unofficial" activities hold? Did it rain cats and dogs on Saturday? How did the website turn out? Was it the best fireworks display ever?

Of course, Blaine was imaginary. We're inclined to leave the last chapter of the Blaine story unwritten. In fact, though, one of us was involved, not so long ago, in a consensus-building effort aimed at accomplishing a very similar outcome: a townwide celebration in a small town in Massachusetts. If anything, the debate in real life was even more passionate and protracted than our rendition of what happened at the BCC's table. (If you think we overplayed the drama in our scenarios, think again!) Yet the ultimate outcome was satisfying to everyone involved. In retrospect, it's hard to imagine how a group committed to majority rule could possibly have generated as good an outcome.

Isn't getting a town's birthday party right relatively small potatoes? Yes. We purposefully chose a small dispute, with a limited number of protagonists and issues, and with no lives at stake, as our primary case. The consequences of getting it wrong in Blaine would have been minor.

But as the stakes go up, as the issues become more important to more people, and as the risks of getting it wrong go up exponentially, doesn't it become increasingly urgent to get the process right?

Doesn't it become increasingly important to break Robert's Rules and turn instead to the proven power of consensus building?

In part 2, we spell out, step-by-step, the CBA alternative to Robert's Rules that groups of all kinds can incorporate into their articles of incorporation.

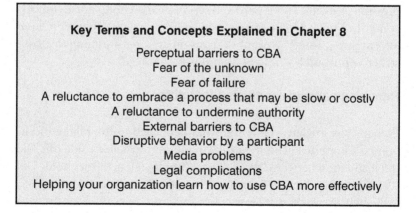

Key Terms and Concepts Explained in Chapter 8

Perceptual barriers to CBA
Fear of the unknown
Fear of failure
A reluctance to embrace a process that may be slow or costly
A reluctance to undermine authority
External barriers to CBA
Disruptive behavior by a participant
Media problems
Legal complications
Helping your organization learn how to use CBA more effectively

Part 2

~

The Five Essential Steps in the Consensus Building Approach (CBA)

Step 1

~

Convening

1.1 Initiate discussion with potential organizer(s)

Anyone can initiate a consensus-building process by raising the idea with the right individual(s) or official(s) in charge. The critical step at the outset is to identify a potential convener—an elected or appointed official or a senior official in the private sector with the formal authority to take action. This person does not need to know very much about CBA in order to play a convening role. At the outset, it is crucial to discuss the advantages and disadvantages of using consensus building, rather than relying exclusively on whatever the usual way of making group decisions might be.

Give the potential convener a copy of *Breaking Robert's Rules*. Explain that they are not being asked to give up any of their formal authority. Point out that the primary reason to use CBA is because it has been proven to be a better way of getting group agreement; in essence, the total value (when generated by consensus) is likely to be greater than the sum of the parts (i.e., the value that the individuals can create on their own). It may take a little longer to get CBA off the ground (i.e., to ensure that all the relevant stakeholders are represented, to get agreement on ground rules, and so on), but the chances are that the overall time it takes to get to an agreement that can be implemented effectively will be less.

1.2   Initiate an assessment

If the convener is willing to explore the idea further, the next step is to initiate the preparation of an **assessment** (sometimes called a conflict assessment). The convener either can tap someone she knows to do this (as long as that person is viewed as nonpartisan or neutral by all the key stakeholders), or the convener can seek help from a professional neutral (i.e., a trained facilitator or mediator). There are professional neutrals listed in almost every telephone book.

Preparation of an assessment involves interviewing the obvious stakeholders (i.e., the first circle) privately and confidentially. This round of interviewees usually suggests a second circle of people to talk to, as well. In the public arena, the fact that an assessment is being prepared should be made public, so people who feel they have an important contribution to make can also ask to be interviewed (a third circle of interviewees). An assessment doesn't need to take very long or cost very much. Once the interviews are done, the assessor needs to write a short synthesis "mapping the conflict"—that is, laying out the major categories of stakeholders and their views on each possible agenda item. This short summary, and a one-page matrix (like the one Connie prepared for Bill on page 58) summarizing the results of the interviews, should be sent to everyone interviewed. Their comments and corrections should be incorporated by the assessor into a final version of the assessment (in which no one who was interviewed is mentioned by name).

1.3   Use the assessment to identify appropriate stakeholder representatives

The assessment should help the assessor spell out for to the convener who the **appropriate people** are to "invite to the table," assuming CBA goes forward. The assessor has to suggest a way to make sure that all relevant stakeholder groups are represented. This is hard in some cases, because some stakeholders may not already be organized. It is almost always possible, however, to find some individual willing to stand in for a hard-to-represent group.

1.4 Finalize commitments to involve appropriate stakeholder representatives if a consensus-building process goes forward

Once all the potential invitees have been identified (by the convener) and the interviewees have had a chance to comment on the draft assessment, the assessor should formulate a potential agenda, work plan, timetable, and budget, and suggest ground rules. These need not be more than one page each in length. (See suggested ground rules in appendix B.) These, too, should be sent in draft to all the stakeholders in preliminary form for their review. They should be asked directly by the assessor if they would agree to participate in a CBA process, if one were initiated by the convener. The attached materials should make it clear what the participants would be asked to accept.

1.5 Decide whether to commit to CBA

Based on the reactions of the key stakeholders, the assessor should be in a position to make a recommendation to the convener about whether to go forward. If the assessor believes that the most important stakeholders will participate, at least in an organizational session, and based on the confidential interviews that—regardless of what may have been said in the newspapers or in other public settings—there is a possibility of finding common ground, then the assessor should tell this to the convener. The convener can decide (either on his own, or with appropriate co-conveners) whether to send a letter of invitation to all relevant stakeholders, urging them to participate.

With the suggested agenda, timetable, budget, and ground rules attached to the invitation, each participant should be able to see what is expected of them. Such invitations usually ask the recipients to commit to attend an organizational meeting at which the convener will asks the parties if they are prepared to work with the person he has suggested as the facilitator. (It could be the same person who prepared the assessment, or someone new.) The parties must then make their own decisions: whether to go forward, who the facilitator should be, and whether to accept or modify the agenda, ground rules, timetable, budget, and even the list of invitees.

1.6 Make sure that those in positions of authority agree to the process

Often the convener needs to contact other elected or appointed officials or members of organizations (and sometimes heads of nongovernmental or business groups) who, while they may not be direct stakeholders, could become involved later on, depending on what the CBA generates by way of proposals. It is usually a good idea to brief those individuals before the process begins to make sure they are willing to support the effort. Final implementation of whatever agreement is produced often requires formal action by such related officials.

Step 2

~

Assigning Roles and Responsibilities

2.1 Specify who will take responsibility for convening, facilitating, recording, moderating or chairing meetings, representing key stakeholder groups, and providing expert advice

At the first meeting, the group as a whole should review its roles and responsibilities. Presumably, all the participants "represent" some larger set of interested stakeholders or constituents. They may also bring special expertise to the discussion. To the extent that one of the participants is unwilling or unable to meet the expectations of the others, with regard to her representational responsibilities, it may be necessary to find a substitute. "Representation" may consist of nothing more than agreeing to serve as a go-between or a two-way channel of information.

In small groups like the Blaine Centennial Committee, it is possible to handle the assignments of these responsibilities in a less formal way, relying on members of the group to take on their assignments periodically. The convener may want to name a member of the group as moderator or chair (for purposes of providing the "outside world" with a point of contact). That role can also be assigned (by the group) to the facilitator.

It is not necessary for the convener to attend every meeting, although she might want to name someone to sit in for her on a regular basis. Technical advisors or experts must be approved by the group as a whole. Often, they are relegated to task forces or subcommittees named by the full group to generate proposals or explore specific topics in advance of full group meetings. Meetings are usually managed by the facilitator. Either a member of the facilitation staff or one of the participants should serve as recorder for each session—keeping a visible written record of key points discussed and preparing a short summary of items of agreement and disagreement to distribute to all the participants soon after each meeting.

2.2 Set rules regarding the involvement of alternates and observers

The credibility of almost any group decision-making process is enhanced when the interactions among the participants are transparent. On the other hand, the work of any deliberative body or team can be made more difficult by the presence of observers. It is important for each CBA group to set clear ground rules regarding which, if any, of its sessions will be open to observers and whether or not the observers will be recognized to speak. In a highly public context, when observers are permitted, it is a good idea to require them to initial written ground rules regarding acceptable behavior and the "rules of engagement" before they are admitted. (This is usually less important inside an organization or a firm.)

Some groups permit all participants to name (at the outset) an alternate empowered to participate on their behalf if they cannot attend a meeting. When this procedure is in effect, it is the participant's obligation to ensure that his alternate is up-to-speed on what has happened thus far, as well as what will be covered at the meeting.

2.3 Finalize the agenda, ground rules, work plan, and budget in written form (for public or organizational review)

At the first meeting, all the participants should take part in a thorough review of the proposed agenda, ground rules, work plan, and budget for the CBA process. Whatever revisions are proposed, a written version should be circulated prior to the second meeting, so that all participants can review them with their relevant constituents or outside actors prior to adopting them at the beginning of the second meeting. There should be a provision in the ground rules allowing any participant to suggest changes in the ground rules, work plan, agenda, or budget at any time with the concurrence of the full group. At the beginning of the second meeting, all participants should be prepared to adopt a final set of ground rules and a work plan.

2.4 Assess options for communicating with the constituencies represented as well as with the community-at-large

Once the discussions are underway, some means of communicating with the broader array of constituents will be needed. How this will be done should be determined at the first meeting. The recorder should send meeting summaries to the participants in a form that they, in turn, can easily distribute to other interested stakeholders. A website may be appropriate in certain circumstances. Written meeting summaries distributed by mail to a continuously-updated mailing list may be most appropriate. The final report or recommendations of the group may need to be distributed in still other forms to ensure the most widespread review possible.

Step 3

~

Facilitating Group
Problem Solving

3.1 Strive for transparency (distribute written summaries of all meetings)

CBA involves not only a set of tools and techniques (like assessment and facilitation) but also a commitment to joint problem solving. Members of any organization or community are not likely to view a joint problem-solving effort as legitimate, however, unless they understand exactly who is meeting, and how well they have handled their assignments. Thus, the legitimacy of any consensus-building effort hinges in large part on the way the process is perceived by those likely to be affected by what is decided.

The legitimacy of both the process and the outcome, in turn, depends on the transparency of the effort. Not only are the written agenda, ground rules, work plan, and budget crucial to the spirit of transparency but so are the written summaries of regular meetings. These should be easily available to anyone interested, along with a draft of the final report, in time for nonparticipants to offer comments before final decisions are made. Unlike traditional minutes, meetings summaries should *not* mention who said what. Rather, they should highlight points of agreement and disagreement, and summarize the evidence and arguments that carried weight with the group.

3.2 Seek expert input when joint fact-finding might be helpful

A great many consensus-building processes involve decisions that hinge, at least in part, on scientific or technical judgments of one kind or another. When technical considerations come into play, all participants should have equal access to the best possible (nonpartisan) advice. It is almost always desirable to avoid the kinds of "dueling experts" (i.e., technical advisors selected by each side to reinforce their interpretation of technical inputs and undermine the technical arguments of others) so common in the courtroom.

Joint fact-finding hinges on the participants working together to (1) spell out the technical matters or questions on which they want advice, (2) select a range of experts to advise the group as a whole, (3) interact with those experts before they begin their work to discuss how they intend to address or answer the group's concerns, and (4) interact with those experts, once they have generated preliminary findings, to discuss the policy implications of their work. A knowledgeable facilitator can often serve as an "interlocutor" between the experts and participants with less technical expertise.

3.3 Create working subcommittees if appropriate

A consensus-building process built around a very full agenda can sometimes be enhanced by appointing subcommittees of interested participants and technical advisors to explore individual or clusters of agenda items, prior to the full group's first effort to address them. Subcommittees should not be given decision-making responsibilities. Rather, they should be offered a setting within which a great deal of technical material can be explored and "homework" on related efforts elsewhere can be reviewed. The goal of subcommittees should be to make the work of the full group easier and to provide a starting point for informed discussion of one or a cluster of agenda items.

3.4 Seek to maximize joint gains through the brainstorming of packages

One of the strongest arguments for the use of CBA—regardless of the scope of the decision-making problem—is that it aims to maximize joint gains in order to create as much value as possible. In other words, it aims to find the best possible way of responding to the conflicting concerns or needs of the stakeholders. The harder the group works to expand the proverbial "pie," the larger the "slice" each is likely to get. The most efficient way to expand the pie is to look for mutually beneficial trades, or what are called **packages**, that give each group more of what is most important to them, in exchange for granting others what they need. This is best accomplished by playing the game of "what-if." One group offers what it thinks will be attractive to the others on a what-if basis, as long as it is guaranteed that what it finds most valuable from the others will be provided in return. Sometimes, the process of packaging is best handled by having the facilitator meet privately with key stakeholders before or between meetings (or during breaks in actual meetings) and then crafting a bundle of proposals, or a package, without saying who specifically offered what to whom.

3.5 Separate inventing from committing

As our colleagues Roger Fisher, Bill Ury, and Bruce Patton have explained in their classic book, *Getting to Yes*, it is hard to get people to brainstorm or play the game of what-if when they are worried that everything they say may be construed as a firm commitment, even before they are ready to make such promises. One of the ground rules in most consensus-building processes, therefore, is that no one should be asked to make firm commitments to a package or a proposal until they are absolutely ready to do so. This ground rule can be summarized in the phrase, "separate inventing from committing," meaning that nothing said during brainstorming can later be thrown back at someone as a promise made earlier.

3.6   Use the help of a skilled facilitator

The steps in the CBA process can get very complicated, especially when there are many parties at the table. Coalitions or alliances sometimes form away from the table. Interpersonal difficulties can impede communication. Outside pressures (usually in the form of unrealistic timetables) can make everyone defensive.

The best way to head off or resolve such difficulties is to have somebody manage the dialogue, someone whose only concern is to make sure that everyone is treated fairly and that the group remains true to its agenda, timetable, and work plan. It is often best to have a professional facilitator play this role, although there are many instances in which someone from inside one of the relevant organizations is trusted enough by all the participants to take on this role. There are growing numbers of accredited professional facilitators (sometimes called dispute resolvers, mediators, or neutrals) who can provide these services on a very reasonable fee-for-service basis.

3.7   Use a single-text procedure

As a CBA process moves along, more and more paper accumulates. Meeting summaries, subcommittee reports, and proposals from individual participants keep appearing. At some point, these all need to be folded into a single-text that everyone can support. While a group may tentatively finish discussing an important item on its agenda in week two, there can be no agreement on anything until the full package is agreed upon by everyone (or almost everyone) at the conclusion of the process. Very often, a statement to this effect is included in the ground rules.

3.8 Modify the agenda, ground rules, and deadlines as you go

As the process of brainstorming proceeds and new packages emerge, it may become clear that the group should consult with additional individuals who were not thought to be central when the process began. Indeed, it may even be appropriate to add additional stakeholder representatives late in the process, depending on whether new issues have emerged. Should this become necessary, the group should revisit its agenda (work plan) and proposed deadlines. It may even need to reconsider some of its ground rules. This is perfectly OK, as long as all such decisions are made collectively and in a transparent way. New members, if they are added, need to be given a chance to review everything that transpired prior to their arrival and to raise any questions that seem important to them. While the group as a whole is unlikely to go back over everything that has emerged at that point—and is contained in the current version of the single-text—they might, in light of the concerns expressed by a new member, be willing to reconsider something that has already been discussed. Remember, no one has made a firm or final commitment until they have reviewed the full package and checked it with their constituents.

Step 4

~

Reaching Agreement

4.1 Seek unanimity on a written package of commitments

Straw polls are a good device for determining how close the participants are to reaching agreement on a single-text (presented by the facilitator or the group leader). Often, it is necessary to add items to the emerging agreement to provide additional benefits to parties that have not yet indicated their approval. This does not mean that everyone involved needs to find the proposed agreement entirely to their liking. Rather, participants should be asked to consider the "full package" in relation to estimated gains and losses they are most likely to get if there is no agreement. While this undoubtedly involves estimates or forecasts of what is likely to happen (rather than something that can be calculated with certainty), it provides the most appropriate point of comparison for each participant. Thus, the objective of CBA is to seek unanimity on a written package that offers all stakeholders something more valuable than what they can expect in the absence of an agreement.

4.2   Use contingent commitments, if appropriate, to deal with uncertainty or risk

Sometimes, there are too many unknowns for a participant in a CBA process to estimate the value to them of the package being proposed. Contingent options can be used to reduce or eliminate such uncertainties. For instance, one participant may only be able to agree with a package if a particular (but unlikely) circumstance can be eliminated entirely as a future possibility. While everyone else in the group is convinced that the concern of that stakeholder is highly unlikely (e.g., there is less than a 1-percent chance that the thing they are worried about will occur), the participant for whom it is the worst of all possibilities may need further assurance before she can sign an agreement. This can be accomplished by including a contingent option in the agreement indicating that if this highly unlikely event does occur, the group will have to get together again and revise the agreement (i.e., all bets would be off).

Sometimes, a table of contingent options can be added to an agreement to win the support of remaining holdouts. Such a table would spell out a wide range of if–then obligations, such as: "if interest rates increase by 5 percent, 6 percent, 7 percent, or more over the next three years, the financial contribution of each participant indicated in the package will be revised as follows." Instead of arguing that interest rates are not likely to increase by 5 percent in the next few years (and reaching no agreement because someone can not be convinced), the group would spell out the revised terms of their agreement under each of these increasingly unlikely circumstances and incorporate the relevant table into the agreement itself.

4.3   Adhere to agreed-upon decision-making procedures

It is important that all participants in a CBA process stick to the procedures they prescribe at the outset. This is important for ensuring the perceived legitimacy of the process in the eyes of the community-at-large. The only changes allowed in the process of decision making should be those made **by the full group**, using a method of amending the ground rules made explicit in the original ground rules.

4.3.1 Ask who can't live with the package

When the facilitator or dialogue leader thinks the stakeholders are close to overwhelming consensus, she should ask, "Who can't live with the package of proposals detailed in the most recent version of the single text?" Anyone who indicates that he can't live with such a package is obliged **under the terms of the ground rules** to explain why they object (i.e., what interests of theirs aren't being met).

4.3.2 Ask those who object to suggest improvements that would make the package acceptable to them without making it unacceptable to others

It is then the obligation of those who object to offer specific "improvements" that would make the agreement acceptable to them without losing the support of others. If a person indicating unhappiness with the package cannot think of any way to do this, others in the group should be encouraged to help. If no one can think of any way of responding to the concerns of the holdout(s), the rest of the group must decide whether to continue with its deliberations or to conclude them, having reached consensus (i.e., seeking unanimity, but settling for overwhelming agreement once it is clear that no one can think of any way to respond to the remaining concerns of the holdout(s) without leaving others worse off).   *Legislature*

4.4 Keep a written record of all agreements

The final written version of the package should indicate who could not live with the draft agreement and why. It should also include in a footnote detailing the ideas or offers considered at the last minute in an effort to respond to the remaining holdout(s).

4.5 Maintain communication with all relevant constituents and the community-at-large

The CBA process is not complete until the final draft of the package, approved by those at the meeting, is circulated by the participants to their constituents and to the convener or convening agencies prior to the final meeting of the stakeholders.

Step 5

~

Holding Parties to Their Commitments

5.1 Seek ratification of the draft agreement by checking back with all relevant constituencies

The CBA process is complete when the stakeholders return one last time to meet face-to-face to review the comments received when the participants took the penultimate (i.e., "next-to-final") draft of the agreement out for review. It may be necessary to modify the package one last time to ensure the support of constituents that the participants are supposed to represent. If major changes to the package are made, however, it may be necessary to go through the final step once again.

5.2 At a final meeting, ask all the stakeholder representatives to indicate their personal support for the package by signing the agreement

While not everyone at the final meeting will have the authority to speak in a legal sense, for the constituents or stakeholders they supposedly represent, it is nevertheless appropriate to ask each individual involved to sign the agreement. Usually, participants are asked to sign a statement that indicates their personal support for the package and their personal promise to work to implement the agreement (and to follow through on any commitment they have made). Sometimes such statements include a sentence indicating that the signatories have, indeed, taken the final draft of the agreement to their constituents for review.

5.3 Present the recommended package of proposals to those with the formal authority to act

The facilitator and/or the group leader (if one has been designated) should meet with the convener or convening agencies to present the final signed package produced by the CBA process. They should explain how the group arrived at its recommendations and make themselves available to answer questions about both the content of the agreement and the procedures that were followed. They should ask those with the authority to act to indicate their reaction to the agreement and to describe the steps they intend to take to follow through on what has been proposed.

5.3.1 Look for ways to make informally negotiated agreements binding

Often it is possible for the convener or convening agencies to transform the proposals from the CBA group into binding mechanisms that will hold everyone to his or her commitments. For example, elected officials can vote on a proposed package and incorporate it into the terms of permits, licenses, regulations, formal policy statements, or legislation. In the corporate context, negotiated agreements can take a contractual form that legally binds the relevant decision makers to adhere to the terms of the agreement. In other situations, the officers of an organization can vote to enact the recommendations produced by the CBA process they set in motion. Including a dispute resolution clause in the agreement is a good way to make sure that unexpected problems do not cause an agreement to unravel but instead trigger a dispute resolution procedure that has been agreed upon ahead of time.

5.4 Reconvene the parties if those in authority can not live with the package to see what changes might be possible

If those in positions of authority determine there are aspects of the package they can not support, it may be desirable to reconvene the stakeholders to discuss further modifications to the agreement, rather than let it languish. Ideally, the draft of the final agreement reviewed by all the constituents should be circulated informally to the relevant convener or convening bodies for their comments, avoiding this kind of impasse.

5.5 Monitor changing circumstances during implementation and reconvene if necessary

Sometimes, negotiated agreements call for periodic review by stakeholders to assess progress toward implementation. This may involve reconvening the full group on the anniversary of their final meeting, or periodic review by a monitoring subcommittee selected by the full group and named in the package. The facilitator is usually designated as the person to bring the participants together to monitor progress or to prepare a revised proposal that would allow the group to amend its final agreement and take account of unexpected events.

Appendices

Appendix A

~

Convincing Others to Use the Consensus Building Approach—A Checklist

Talking to Potential Participants

For someone with a lot at stake in an upcoming organizational or community battle, CBA can be a lifesaver. Here's how we try to convince them that this is true.

The pitch

We can do better. Our current approach to handling controversial decisions isn't working very well. Remember our last battle royal? We spent a lot of time disagreeing with each other, and then we voted. While it may seem fair to go with what the majority wants, this rarely produces the best possible agreement, and it certainly doesn't guarantee that all the relevant knowledge available will be taken into account. No one feels responsible for coming up with something that's good for anyone else; all they want to do is meet their own needs. There's got to be a better way, and it turns out there is. It's called the "consensus-building approach," or CBA. It doesn't cost more or take extra time. Based on what others have found, it is not difficult to switch to CBA. In fact, even if our articles of incorporation require us to operate by Robert's Rules, we can still use CBA.

There's nothing to lose. What do we have to lose? We can try it, and if it doesn't work, or if we don't like it for any reason, we can switch back. Let's pilot-test it. We don't have to make long-term organizational changes to use CBA. If we like the results, we can look into making it permanent. For now, though, let's just try it. The first step is to prepare an assessment: have someone complete confidential interviews with all the key stakeholders. This will give us a "map" of the conflict we are facing. It will also help us get the right people to the table, with an appropriate agenda, ground rules, and work plan. Wouldn't you agree that we should find out what we're up against, and determine whether CBA might be able to help us?

We'll actually improve the odds of getting something done. The thing about CBA that we find so attractive is that it produces a written agreement that everyone is really committed to implement. Things are much more likely to get done when everyone has been consulted and has had a hand in generating a plan of action. CBA ensures that whatever agreement emerges is based on the best possible information or technical advice. Our typical way of doing business often ends up with groups challenging the legitimacy of the numbers produced by others. Once the experts get into it, nobody has any idea what to believe. If CBA can help us achieve an informed consensus, we're much more likely to get a good result.

Here's what's involved. There are five steps in the CBA process. The first is called **Convening**. It ensures that those with formal authority are ready to back a CBA process. It also involves preparing an assessment that will bring the right participants to the table. The second involves **Assigning Roles and Responsibilities**. In a CBA process, someone has to facilitate, someone else has to keep track of what's being said, and so on. The third step in the CBA process is **Facilitating Group Problem Solving**. This is where brainstorming comes in. The fourth step, **Reaching Agreement**, involves making sure that consensus has actually been reached. The final step involves **Holding Parties (and the groups they represent) to Their Commitments**.

Elicit their concerns

It's not enough to make the same pitch about CBA to all potential participants. At its core, consensus building involves listening to each stakeholder's concerns and trying to tailor an appropriate response. Not surprisingly, we advocate listening closely to what each participant's concerns might be and then responding accordingly. Here are some of the concerns we have heard and our responses to them:

Suppose they say, "It's a waste of time. Those in power will do what they want anyway."

Our response is: You are going to have to put some time into this decision process because the issue is important to you. You *care* about what's being decided. However skeptical you might be about the willingness of those in power to listen, you are going to try to get your views across. So you might as well try this new way of doing things. It can't be any worse, right? If those in power agree to a consensus-building process, you won't object. If they agree to go forward, they will be offering you a chance to participate as a full-fledged partner. If they are going to operate by consensus, that would mean that your voice would carry more weight, not less. What do you have to lose?

Suppose they say, "We think we're going to do OK under the old rules."

Our response is: The thing about CBA is that it seeks to help every participant do at least as well as they would if there were no agreement. So if you think you are going to do pretty well under the old rules (and you are being realistic about that), you can demand that the others around the table help you do at least as well under CBA. Or, you should say no when asked if you can live with the proposed agreement. Nothing lost there, right?

Suppose they say, "We don't want to empower the opposition."

Our response is: Look at it the other way around. Do you really think that refusing to listen to what someone has to say will delegitimize their views? In many instances, freezing someone out merely lends credibility to their claims that they are being mistreated or ignored. That kind of treatment often generates more sympathy for their plight. You don't empower someone by letting them have their say and then explaining why you don't agree with their views.

Suppose they say, "We don't want to forfeit our rights."

Our response is: Participating in a CBA process in no way requires a participant to relinquish one's rights. You can participate in the early rounds of a consensus-building effort and then walk away, at whatever point in the process, to pursue your legal options. You might even participate all the way to the end of a CBA process and then refuse to sign the agreement, because you felt that your interests were not being served. This would *increase*, rather than decrease, the legitimacy of your subsequent efforts to exercise your rights.

Suppose they say, "We're not skilled at using this new approach."

Our response is: It is not hard to pursue your interests in a CBA process. It's very informal. All you have to do is state your interests, listen to what others have to say, and speak your mind. If you want additional training, a skilled facilitator can offer a short course to any and all participants.

Suppose they say, "It will take forever to get agreement."

Our response is: Almost every CBA process operates within deadlines approved by the full group. If the participants want to give themselves more time, they can. If the group doesn't finish within the time it originally allotted itself, and if it doesn't want to extend the deadlines, its members can revert to their usual way of making decisions.

Talking to potential conveners

Potential conveners are typically people in leadership roles. They will usually want to talk about the long-term implications of getting involved in a CBA process. Because the concerns of potential conveners are different from those of potential participants, the "pitch" to a potential convener needs to be different.

The pitch

There's got to be a better way.   Most groups and organizations have a hard time making strategic choices or adjusting to change—especially when there are widely differing views within the group or organization about what ought to be done. The formal procedures in place for making most group decisions tend to produce happy winners and unhappy losers. CBA offers a better way of getting everyone involved, so that whatever is decided is seen as being in the best interests of the organization as a whole.

Take the long view.   This will make things easier in the future, as well. Most participants or stakeholders have the luxury of focusing primarily on what happens in the short run. But potential conveners have the obligation to think in the longer term. The results of a CBA process are, in fact, easier to implement than decisions made by majority rule or other elaborate Robert's Rules-type procedures. When clear reasons are given about *why* a decision has been made, those who prefer a different course of action will find it easier to live with the result. Because CBA seeks to include everyone in the decisions that are being made, it leaves relationships intact. This makes it easier to work together over the long term.

It won't cost more or take longer to get something done.   There's a widespread assumption that it takes a long time to build consensus, and when decisions have to made quickly (which is almost always the case), consensus building isn't appropriate. Of course, this focuses solely on getting the decision made but not implemented. Decisions that are made autocratically (or behind closed doors) are often much more difficult to implement. If we ask, "Does it take longer to actually implement decisions made by consensus, as compared to those that are imposed by someone "at the top" or by a bare majority, the answer is usually no.

A willingness to try CBA will show that you are a real leader.   As a leader, you have to think about the reactions you'll get if you endorse a CBA process. In our experience, leaders of groups, organizations, and agencies of all kinds have discovered that by involving people directly in decisions that affect them, they increase the loyalty of those individuals. While it's true that authoritative leaders (i.e., those who make decisions on behalf of others) are sometimes admired for their strength of character, over time such leaders disempower others. But facilitative leaders, such as those who support CBA, have other strengths. They build organizational and community capacity by requiring the people they work with to share responsibility for making difficult choices that take account of the common good (and not just individual needs).

Your formal authority remains the same.   Sometimes potential conveners are worried that by supporting CBA they are relinquishing their statutory or formal authority. Nothing could be farther from the truth. The participants in a CBA process are expected to prepare a package of proposals. The ultimate authority, however, remains in the hands of the convener. Most conveners are eager to know what the reactions of various groups will be to policies they might adopt (before they make firm commitments). CBA provides that information without undercutting the convener's formal authority.

Elicit their concerns

Suppose they say, "It looks like I'll be tying my hands before
I know what I want to do."

Our response is: That's really not the case. Every CBA process begins with a mandate from the convener to the participants. That mandate makes clear that the charge to the group is to develop a package of proposals that the convener will take under advisement. Obviously, if the convener says that she is likely to support something that has the unanimous approval of all relevant stakeholders (and takes account of the important constraints), the participants are more likely to take the task seriously. The convener reserves the right to reject even a unanimous agreement, although she will be expected to explain her reasons for doing so.

Suppose they say, "This makes it even easier for my enemies
to get in front of the camera."

Our response is: CBA will require anyone who opposes you to go public with their concerns, to give reasons that justify the positions they take, and to offer proposals that meet not just their interests but the interests of all relevant groups. If you have enemies, what better way to force them out into the open (so they can no longer work against you behind the scenes)?

Suppose they say, "I'll be setting a precedent that
I'm not sure I want to set."

Our response is: Each CBA process stands alone. Just because CBA is used in one situation does not mean it should always be used in similar situations. Indeed, that's why each CBA process begins with an assessment. Only after a close look at the particulars is it possible to determine whether CBA is appropriate, and if so, how it should be structured. No precedent is set just because a decision to use CBA is made in one particular situation.

Talking to the media

The biggest mistake that most people make when talking to the media is that they forget the cardinal rule: **Anything you say can (and probably will) be used against you in the court of public opinion.** Any snippet, any sound bite, is fair game. It can easily be taken out of context and turned against you. Remember, the media are looking for a juicy conflict, because that is what sells papers and attracts eyeballs. So from the standpoint of a reporter, CBA presents some real challenges, beginning with the fact that it doesn't generate very interesting headlines. (STAKEHOLDERS MEET TO WORK OUT THEIR DIFFERENCES! EVERYONE IS BETTER OFF!) So, when we initiate a new consensus-building process, we approach the editorial staff (rather than the news staff) and try to make three points:

1. **We will be trying a new way of doing things—a more cooperative approach.** Consensus building has been tried in a lot of other places with great success. CBA, as long as it's done right, allows stakeholders to select their own representatives—the people they most want "at the table." Because there is a skilled facilitator involved, and appropriate ground rules are followed, the results are likely to be pretty good. CBA puts a premium on brainstorming and problem solving, not behind-closed-door deal making. Considerable effort is made to find creative solutions that meet the interests of everyone involved. Of course, the product is only a proposal to those with the formal authority to act. Most of the time, however, elected and appointed officials are pleased to know what they can do that has the support of everyone concerned. If CBA fails, the worst that happens is that the parties will fall back on their usual way of making decisions.

2. **This new way is much more out in the open. It's easier for everyone who wants to participate to get involved.** The thing about CBA is that is it totally transparent. Meetings are open to the public (although observers have to follow certain ground rules). Meeting summaries are available to anyone who wants them. Nothing is decided until a written proposal is circulated to all constituencies for their comments. Anyone who wants to contribute can do so. The people with responsibility for making final decisions still have to go through their usual process; only this time—before they act—they have a written proposal (or what's called a "package") in front of them. The package will come as close as possible to meeting the most important interests of everyone concerned.

3. **The outcome of a CBA process is likely to yield better results for all parties than they would get if they did things in the usual way.** CBA is not about compromise. It's about thinking creatively and finding mutu-

ally beneficial "trades" that create as much value as possible. This can only happen if people work together in a new way. Of course, this takes a different kind of leadership and sometimes requires more work than would otherwise be the case. Nevertheless, most people think it's worth the extra time and effort if the chances of getting what they want are enhanced.

Appendix B

~

Suggested Ground Rules

Ground Rules Governing the Behavior of Participants

1. **Only one person will speak at a time**, and no one will interrupt when another person is speaking.
2. Each person agrees to candidly identify **the interests of the constituency she represents.**
3. Each person will **express his own views**, rather than speaking for others at the table or attributing motives to them.
4. Each person will **avoid grandstanding** (i.e., making extended comments or asking repeated questions), so that everyone has a fair chance to speak and to contribute.
5. **No one will make personal attacks**. Participants agree to challenge ideas, not people. If a personal attack is made, the facilitator will ask the participants to refrain from personal attacks. If personal attacks continue, the facilitator may ask the group to take a break to "cool off."
6. Each person will make every effort to **stay on track with the agenda** and to move the deliberations forward.
7. Each person will seek to **focus on the merits of what is being said**, making a good faith effort to understand the concerns of others. Clarifying questions are encouraged; rhetorical questions and disparaging comments are discouraged.
8. Each person will seek to follow a **"no surprises"** rule—voicing her concerns whenever they arise. In this way, no one will be taken off-guard late in the deliberations when someone suddenly raises an objection.

9. Each person will seek to **identify options or proposals that represent common ground**, without glossing over or minimizing legitimate disagreements. Each participant agrees to do his best to take account of the interests of the group as a whole.

10. Each person **reserves the right to disagree** with any proposal and **accepts responsibility for offering alternatives** that accommodate her interests as well as the interests of others.

11. Each person agrees to **keep the constituencies he or she represents informed** about the issues and options under discussion and to **seek their input and advice on any recommendations** that emerge.

12. Each person will **speak to the media about only his own views.** No member will speak on behalf of other participants or the group as a whole.

Ground Rules for Group Decision Making

1. Each person agrees to fully and consistently **participate in the process unless that person withdraws.** If participants are thinking of withdrawing, they agree to explain their reasons for doing so and to give the others a chance to accommodate their concerns.

2. **Consensus is reached** when the participants agree that they can "live with" the package being proposed. Some participants may not agree completely with every feature of the package as proposed, but they do not disagree enough to warrant opposition to the whole package.

3. The following scale will be used periodically by the facilitator to test whether consensus has been reached. **Using straw votes**, participants should express their level of comfort and commitment by indicating:

    a. Wholeheartedly agree
    b. Good idea
    c. Supportive
    d. Reservations—would like to talk
    e. Serious concerns—must talk
    f. Cannot be part of the decision—must block it

    If all the participants fall between *a* and *c*, consensus on the item under discussion will be assumed. When someone falls between *d* and *f*, that person must state concerns clearly and offer a constructive alternative.

4. If the stakeholder **representatives can not reach consensus**, they agree to document the agreements they have reached, clarify the reasons for disagreeing, and indicate how the remaining disagreements might be resolved.

5. The participants will consider their **"fallback" option if no agreement can be reached**, including mechanisms that provide incentives for the participants to continue trying to reach agreement. Fallback options include:

a. identifying issues requiring further research and suspending deliberations until that research has been completed;
b. agreeing to switch to a super-majority voting rule (e.g., something
like a 75-percent or 80-percent majority would be required);
c. seeking a recommendation from the convener or an independent expert regarding possible ways of resolving their remaining disagreements.
This might provide a "reality check" that encourages one or more parties to come back to the table with more realistic expectations;
d. including a minority report;
e. letting the authorized decision maker (the convener) impose a decision.

Appendix C

∽

Being a Good Facilitator

A good facilitator is ready and willing to take on the following tasks:

- *Assessing*, with the participants, the situation and determining whether CBA is appropriate;
- *Designing*, with the participants, ground rules, a work plan, and other mechanisms to guide the process;
- *Managing* relationships and communication among the participants (and with their constituencies);
- *Training* the participants in negotiation and consensus-building skills (if they request such assistance);
- *Facilitating* meetings, assisting in preparation for meetings, and preparing summaries of meetings;
- *Representing* the process to the media and the world-at-large;
- *Respecting confidentiality* in all interactions with stakeholder participants and with the convener;
- *Enforcing* the ground rules agreed upon by the participants, including confronting any participant (or observer) who is not abiding by the ground rules;
- *Mediating* specific issues, including shuttling back and forth among the participants clarifying interests and positions;
- *Fact-finding* in relation to a specific issue in circumstances where the participants are comfortable with that arrangement—including organizing expert panels to conduct the research;

- **Preparing** a written draft ("single-text") containing the final package of proposals and sounding out the participants on their willingness to "live with" the agreement;
- **Ensuring** that the participants check back with their constituents and sign a statement indicating their personal support for implementation of the agreement;
- **Monitoring** implementation and the need for possible modifications of the agreement;
- **Reconvening** the parties, following procedures spelled out in the agreement.

Appendix D

❦

General Robert Goes to Town Meeting

Imagine a New England town meeting— sometimes called the purest form of democracy—in which Robert's Rules are strictly observed.

As General Robert envisioned the meeting, all of the several hundred people in attendance arrive having studied the "Order of Precedence of Motions and the Table of Rules Relating to Motions." They all have their personal copies of *Robert's Rules of Order* close at hand for easy reference. The meeting does its business in strict conformance with the rules, with everyone understanding exactly what is going on, knowing how and when to make themselves heard in a procedurally correct way.

But what *really* happens at a typical town meeting? Almost nobody understands Robert's Rules or even knows that they apply. The moderator may have a copy of the *Rules* at the podium, or may not. Town counsel, over at the side table, probably has one in her brief case but probably hopes she doesn't actually have to take it out.

Sooner or later—usually when the proceedings get hot, and tempers are wearing thin—someone stands up and shouts, "Point of procedure!" Or, "Point of order!" Or, "Point of privilege!" The speaker, using odd language that no one is able to follow, then makes a confusing assertion about procedure, privilege, or whatever.

Almost no one knows exactly what to do next. There's a huddle at the front of the room. Most of the town meeting members wait in confusion while the town leaders try to figure out what's procedurally correct. The minutes tick by. Finally, a decision is rendered, and the meeting starts again.

The first time this happens, town meeting members may be tolerant of the delay and disruption. The fifteenth or fiftieth time, they aren't. They begin to feel, rightly or wrongly, that the meeting is being "hijacked" by people who are deliberately raising unnecessary procedural points. They put pressure on the moderator to muzzle the parliamentary gadflies and "get on with business."

The same thing happens when someone rises for the fifteenth time to amend a motion on the floor, or worse, amend the amendment to the motion on the floor. Gradually, the *substance* of the original motion gets lost amid all of the parliamentary maneuvering. Again, the moderator comes under pressure to limit the time that a single member can chew up with procedural objections and amendments. A rising chorus of voices demands that the group be allowed to vote on the question at hand.

Think about it. Assuming that the gadfly knows his stuff, he is *only playing by the rules.*

What if, as General Robert advocated, the entire town meeting played by those rules? Process would win out over substance. Most likely, the meeting would never end. And if it did, most of the decisions reached would be challenged at a later meeting.

What if the moderator and town counsel, huddling at the front of the room, unfairly manipulate a process that almost no one understands? That's too much power to put in the hands of one or two people.

And what if, by muzzling the gadflies, the moderator actually prevents important ideas from getting heard? If that happens, the outcome won't be as good as it should have been. Again, the decisions reached will be unstable and may even be viewed as illegitimate. Before people leave the meeting, they will be plotting how to (1) elect a moderator more to their liking, and (2) win enough additional votes to get what they want at the next town meeting.

Town meeting is an extreme case, but the same dynamics tend to arise in other settings. Let's imagine that a local nonprofit corporation—say, a group trying to build affordable housing in an affluent suburb—has a board of directors with seven members. And imagine that this group, which runs its meetings according to Robert's Rules, makes a highly controversial decision by a four-to-three vote. Split decisions, which require zoning changes and large investments of money down the road, will spark continuing public debate and may well be overturned.

Nevertheless, the debate at the table is surprisingly perfunctory. It's pretty clear that a deal was cut ahead of time and that the four board members in the majority never intended to listen seriously to what the minority wanted. But they're *careful.* They observe Robert's Rules scrupulously, so that they can't be tripped up procedurally after the fact.

So what do the losers do in a case like this? They drag their feet as much as possible during implementation, they bring the same issue up again and again at every possible juncture, just as often as the rules allow. Meanwhile, they organize, mobilize, and wait for a seat to open on the board. When they finally succeed at grabbing that open seat, they push for reconsideration of the controversial decision at the first opportunity. And, if they succeed at reversing the decision, then months or even years of hard work may be undone.

Appendix E

◇

Consensus Building
in the Workplace

In our introduction, we described a small-engine plant with product-introduction woes. In that example—taken from real life, albeit thinly disguised—we saw a senior vice president fly into Sacramento from out of town to "read the riot act" to the management and union leaders at that plant.

Obviously, this is not the best way to undertake a consensus-building effort in a business setting (although when our senior VP announced that he was looking for solutions rather than scapegoats, he was pointing in the right direction.) But there *are* ways to go about this. Even though the hierarchy in most businesses is quite different from the structure of other organizations, our experience suggests that CBA in the private sector is not only possible but profitable. Internal conflict in organizations tends to waste resources and undermine effectiveness. Consensus building—as modified to fit the private sector—minimizes (or at least structures) these conflicts.

In the following pages, you will see references to methods and processes that have been described in previous chapters. It is important to grasp these methods and processes before attempting to follow the steps outlined below.

Why do conflicts arise inside an organization?

Before we can address the issue of how to resolve conflicts in a business setting, it is worth agreeing on the reasons why disputes arise in the first place. There are at least five such reasons. First, organizations today are flatter and more networked than ever before. This means that many managers find themselves trying to meet responsibilities that extended beyond their authority—a primary cause of internal tension.

Second, organizations are more matrixed and team-based. Pressures applied to break down silos and force people (who may not agree on much of anything) to work together tend to trigger stiff resistance.

Third, many organizations find that increasingly they are forced to adapt to rapidly shifting environmental constraints. Since resistance to change is inevitable, efforts to promote such adjustments often provoke obstructionist behavior.

Fourth, some organizations are struggling to manage increasing diversity, as their workforces incorporate staff with conflicting styles and unfamiliar cultural attributes. This is an honorable goal, but it certainly can lead to conflict.

And fifth, most organizations are under extreme pressure to "do more with less." This means that subunits often find themselves competing for scare resources.

Because these five sources of internal pressure are unavoidable, managers must find ways of addressing conflict inside their organizations more effectively.

The conventional wisdom and the alternative

The conventional wisdom about the best way of dealing with internal conflict puts primary responsibility in the hands of top management. Senior managers (who have plenty of clout) should simply insist that employees put aside their personal differences for the good of the company. Managers should work to make sure that roles and responsibilities are clarified because in most cases—according to the conventional wisdom—conflict is the result of a lack of clarity about lines of authority or turf overlap. And at the end of the day, senior managers should exercise their authority; in other words, they should actually "tell everyone what to do."

This approach puts a premium on steering from above and implicitly assumes that pressure from the top will produce the desired result. Unfortunately, this approach usually treats only *symptoms*, rather than underlying causes. It follows the path of least resistance, rather than addressing the real sources of difficulty. Thus, it often fails. Worst of all, the traditional approach rarely prompts the kind of organizational learning that would help head off similar kinds of problems in the future.

Two organizations with which one of the authors of this book, Lawrence Susskind, is associated—the Program on Negotiation (PON) at Harvard Law School and the Consensus Building Institute (CBI)—have for many years offered a workshop that presents a different approach to managing conflict inside organizations: one that foregoes "steering from above" in favor of CBA, which seeks to involve all relevant stakeholders. They offer an integrated model for dealing with internal conflict that stresses: (1) diagnosing the sources of conflict, (2) building consensus from differences, (3) selling agreements and overcoming resistance, and (4) pushing back on the organization (to encourage institutional learning).

This approach is detailed in the following pages. In our experience, it is much more likely to get to good solutions and build lasting organizational capabilities than traditional top-down methods.

Diagnosing the sources of conflict

There are a great many well-documented instances of internal conflict that arise when subunits are asked to accept centrally imposed changes in business practices— jettisoning their current computer architecture, for example, in favor of a new company-wide system; or altering lines of authority to take account of a new matrix management approach.

Let's look at a case in point. In one national investment firm, sales people who sold particular investment products on a national basis (and reported to a designated national product manager responsible for calculating their annual bonuses) were told that in addition, they now had to report to new regional account managers, who would also have a hand in determining their bonuses.

The sales staff was conflicted. Their loyalties were split. Now they were expected to be equally attentive to the concerns of new regional account managers, installed at the same organizational level as the national product managers, who wanted to reprogram the way they allocated their time and effort. Conflicting loyalties led to a sales staff rebellion.

Getting the parties to agree that there is a problem

The first step in tending to an internal conflict of this kind is to get all the parties to agree on the scope and source of the problem. In the financial services case, this had to be done carefully because anxieties were already running high. Let's look at the steps that this firm followed.

An external consultant experienced in consensus building—and hired by the senior VP for sales—met privately with the national product managers, the regional account managers, and a cross-section of the most experienced sales staff. Based on these interviews, the consultant offered a preliminary assessment of the situation. The consultant's goal was to frame his analysis in a way that held out hope that the problem could be resolved to everyone's benefit. The consultant used a variety of benchmarks to ground his assessment in terms that everyone found meaningful (i.e., by tracing changes in the pattern and level of product and regional sales following the introduction of the new matrix management approach).

He demonstrated that it ought to be possible for everyone involved to come out ahead (i.e., national product sales could be increased by increasing regional sales, thereby increasing commissions for all sales staff). Top management encouraged the consultant to design a relatively brief CBA process aimed at sorting out the tensions between the national product managers and the regional account managers that were undermining sales.

Authorizing the problem-solving effort

For the problem solving effort to proceed effectively, it was necessary for the consultant to secure a range of highly visible endorsements for the CBA. In this instance, that meant organizing a one-day meeting at which top management made it clear that it was committed to finding a solution that met everyone's interests. It also meant locating the requisite resources to support the consensus-building effort.

Preparing a conflict assessment

In PON/CBI's integrated model, the key is to begin with a formal assessment. So, after meeting privately with all the key stakeholders, the consultant produced a "map" of the conflict listing all the concerns raised in the confidential interviews with more than twenty-five of the key players. The written ten-page draft (which did not attribute comments to anyone by name) was sent to everyone who had been interviewed to ensure that all concerns had been incorporated accurately. Thus, the goal of securing stakeholder endorsement of the assessment findings was achieved.

The assessment included a matrix, with key concerns listed along the top and categories of stakeholder listed down the side. In each cell of the matrix, stakeholder group ideas regarding that particular problem or issue were enumerated (along with a sense of the urgency that each group attached to that issue). Based on the interview results, the consultant prepared a one-month work plan (including some fact-finding that might be helpful) and a set of suggested ground rules to guide the problem-solving effort.

Mobilizing stakeholders to participate

Once the assessment (and the proposal for going forward) had been reviewed by all the stakeholders, each of the three key groups (national product managers, regional account managers, and sales staff) caucused to clarify its interests and identify two or three people to "represent" them. The consultant organized a preliminary meeting of these nine individuals. Thus, each stakeholder group had not only a hand in selecting its own "representatives" to participate in the problem-solving effort but also a role in laying out that group's agenda.

Building consensus from differences

The consultant facilitated three half-day meetings over a period of three weeks. The goal was to formulate a "package" of ideas or strategies that would help make the matrix management plan work for everyone. The consultant relied on four key ideas:

Understanding each other's interests and values. He began by prompting each of the group "representatives" to clarify her interests—the kinds of things important to them in rank order. He interrupted when they presented positions, rather than interests, pressing them to say **why** they were taking the positions they did.

Brainstorming options.   Once each group made its interests clear, the consultant prompted them to suggest possible ways of meeting interests on all sides. For example, how could members of the sales staff be responsive to both their national product managers *and* their regional accounts manager at the same time? What communication and coordination between the two sides of the matrix might best help the sales staff achieve their quarterly targets? Might it be possible to develop a clearer formula for allocating sales staff time to national and regional sales efforts? Multiple ideas were generated on these and related topics, although no commitments were sought.

At one point there was a factual disagreement on the content of the employment contracts of the sales staff. A subcommittee was chosen by the full group to investigate and produce data for the full group. Joint fact-finding made it much more likely that all the stakeholders would accept the analysis that came back.

Packaging draft agreements.   Using a single-text procedure, the facilitator generated a summary statement pulling together the best ideas from the brainstorming sessions. Justifications were provided for each proposal, both in terms of how they would meet the interests of each stakeholder group and how they would produce the best possible result for the company as a whole.

Getting check-offs.   Finally, it came time to see whether the full group would accept the draft agreement. Lingering concerns on the part of one of the regional account managers were addressed. As the group reached its previously agreed deadline, the facilitator asked, "Who can't live with this final version of the agreement?" He had made it clear, as it had been stated in the ground rules, that he would seek unanimity but settle for overwhelming agreement. All but one of the nine participants agreed to sign the proposal to forward to the senior VP for sales.

The facilitation role played by the consultant was important. In fact, the only way the group was able to reach agreement was through the consultant's skilled intervention. He kept the group on task (within the confines of the work plan and timetable to which they had all agreed). He prodded them between meetings to be sure that they came prepared and stayed in touch with the constituents they ostensibly represented. He provided an authoritative voice for the group effort so that no one felt she could go around the process to advance her own interests. Finally, the consultant agreed to drive the follow-up activities spelled out in the agreement.

Overcoming resistance

Even though they had reached an agreement, the task force's work wasn't done. Our colleague, Professor Deborah Kolb, highlights three important tasks that still remained. First, they had to cultivate support for their proposal. Second, they had to present the agreement in a strategic way, taking account of other things going on in the organization at the same time. Third, they had to build a coalition to support the changes they were suggesting. Let's look at each of these tasks in turn.

Cultivating support

Kolb talks about using **appreciative moves** to cultivate support for the agreement reached by the task force. Appreciative moves consist of conversations that acknowledge the concerns of others (and legitimize their stories). In this spirit, the task force members and the consultant spent considerable time meeting one-on-one with people who were not directly involved but who might have questions about the proposals that the task force had generated. They were ready with face-saving suggestions for those who might be opposed to specific ideas in the task force report.

Framing agreements in strategic terms

Kolb also talks about using **process moves** to keep ideas on the agenda even in the face of opposition. These emphasize "small victories," even before the full task force report was implemented. In this case, the fact that the contending groups within the company were working together to solve the problem was emphasized again and again in all kinds of conversations. Everybody realized that they would benefit if quarterly sales rebounded as a result of the work of the task force.

Building a coalition to support change

Finally, Kolb suggests using **power moves** to build a supporting coalition. In this case, the task force was able to convert a number of "fence sitters" to supporters by arguing that the consensus-building approach, if successful, might well be used to solve other problems that had not yet been addressed successfully. As supporters of the task force report made themselves known, blockers were isolated. In this fashion, a winning coalition was created.

Pushing back on the organization

Even with the endorsement of top management, the efforts of the task force were still not completed. It is not sufficient to fix the problem if it just going to occur again and again. To the extent possible, organizational learning should be encouraged so that the root cause of a conflict (in this case, insufficient preparation prior to the imposition of a change as radical as the new matrix-management approach) might be avoided in the future.

Diagnosing/learning focused on the root causes of the conflict

Organizational learning, when it does occur, is typically driven by dissatisfaction with current circumstances and a desire to do better in the future. The conflict addressed by the task force offered a terrific opportunity for the organization to learn how to handle such conflicts more effectively (before they blossomed into full-fledged rebellion). According to Professor Bert Spector, "Learning can not be imposed from the top. It needs to proceed from a shared diagnosis of root causes." In this case, it was possible to name the problem: a rather typical (for this organization) top-down imposition of a substantial change in managerial structure without adequate consultation or attention to the concerns of those likely to be affected.

Promoting new patterns of behavior

The key to the agreement reached by the task force was specific changes in reporting relationships, as well as new "rules of thumb" for allocating sales force time to both national product sales and regional accounts. The task force recommended that these changes be officially monitored on a quarterly basis and that responsibility for producing a published analysis of how the new arrangements were working be assigned to a specific member of the task force. Thus, new patterns of behavior would be carefully benchmarked and monitored until everyone could be sure they were in place. It is impossible to promote new patterns of behavior without such credible monitoring to ensure that desired changes in behavior are taking place.

Reinforcing new patterns of behavior

Of course, the *real* reason that the sales staff was in rebellion was that the new matrix management approach made it extremely unclear how (or if) each sales person could earn the same or increased commissions. No one knew the relative clout of the national sales managers versus the regional account managers when it came time to figure bonuses. Thus, the sales staff did not know how its best interests could be served (while meeting corporate requirements). In the end, the task force recommended not only that each sales person negotiate a single "annual sales contract" signed by the two managers to whom they reported under the reorganization, but they also suggested an appeals process for sales staffers who felt that their performance was not properly assessed when it came time to allocate bonuses.

Until the new management system was in place long enough to see how it would work, anxiety levels remained high. While some in the company thought that uncertainty of this kind would spur greater sales efforts, others knew that this would not be the case. The work of the task force provided a means of reducing the anxiety associated with managerial innovation by allowing key stakeholders a chance to help frame the necessary changes required to make it work. The conflict was viewed by the task force not just as a problem to be resolved in the short run but as an opportunity for the company to learn how other management changes in the future might be implemented more effectively.

The good news is that top management recognized both opportunities, commended the task force for its work, and vowed to adopt CBA in connection with other controversial managerial changes. Indeed, in many companies, new approaches to internal dispute resolution are now being implemented that build on the idea of consensus building. These go by many names—IDR (internal dispute resolution), ODR (organizational dispute resolution) or in very large organizations like the World Bank and the United Nations "integrated dispute resolution"—and involve consensual decision-making, ombudsmen, mediation, and in addition to conventional collective bargaining, a mutual gains approach to contract negotiation. Many require substantial modifications in the way that human resource professionals do their job. All require a commitment on the part of top management to use CBA whenever possible.

Appendix F

~

Handy Guide to the
Five Essential Steps in the Consensus
Building Approach (CBA)

1. Convening

1.1 Initiate discussion
1.2 Initiate a project assessment
1.3 Use the assessment to identify appropriate stakeholder representatives
1.4 Finalize commitments to involve appropriate stakeholder representatives
1.5 Decide whether to commit to a CBA
1.6 Make sure that those in positions of authority agree to the process

2. Assigning Roles and Responsibilities

2.1 Specify who will take responsibility for convening, facilitating, recording, chairing meetings, representing key stakeholders, and providing expert advice
2.2 Set rules regarding the involvement of alternates and observers
2.3 Finalize the agenda, ground rules, work plan, and budget in writing
2.4 Assess options for communicating with the constituencies represented, as well as with the community-at-large

3. Facilitating Group Problem Solving

3.1 Strive for transparency
3.2 Seek expert input when joint fact-finding might be helpful
3.3 Create working subcommittees if appropriate
3.4 Seek to maximize joint gains through the brainstorming of the packages
3.5 Separate inventing from committing
3.6 Use the help of a skilled facilitator
3.7 Use a single-text procedure
3.8 Modify the agenda, ground rules, and deadlines as you go

4. Reaching Agreement

4.1 Seek unanimity on a written package of commitments
4.2 Use contingent commitments, if appropriate
4.3 Adhere to agreed upon decision-making procedures
  4.3.1 Ask who can't live with the package
  4.3.2 Ask those who object to suggest improvements that would make the package acceptable to them without making it unacceptable to others
4.4 Keep a written record of all agreements
4.5 Maintain communication with all relevant constituents and the comunity-at-large

5. Holding Parties to Their Commitments

5.1 Seek ratification by checking back with all relevant constituencies
5.2 Ask all stakeholder representatives to indicate their personal support by signing the agreement
5.3 Present the recommended package to those with formal authority to act
  5.3.1 Look for ways to make informally negotiated agreements binding
5.4 Reconvene the parties if those in authority cannot live with the package
5.5 Monitor changing circumstances during implementation and reconvene if necessary

Appendix G

~

Background Readings

Robert's Rules of Order
Robert, Henry M. III, William Evans, Daniel Honemann, and Thomas Balch. 2000. *Robert's Rules of Order*. Rev. ed. Cambridge, MA: Perseus.
Sylvester, Nancy. 2004. *Complete Idiot's Guide to Robert's Rules*. New York: Alpha/Penguin.

Majority Rule and Voting
Brams, Steven, and Alan Taylor. 1996. *Fair Division: From Cake-Cutting to Dispute Resolution*. Cambridge: Cambridge Univ. Press.
Brandenburger, Adam, and Barry Nalebuff. 1996. *Co-Opetition: A Revolution Mindset That Combines Competition and Cooperation*. New York: Bantam, Doubleday, Dell.
Raiffa, Howard, with John Richardson and David Metcalfe. 2003. *Negotiation Analysis: The Science and Art of Collaborative Decision Making*. Cambridge, MA: Belknap Press.

Consensus Building and Collaboration
Gray, Barbara. 1989. *Collaborating: Finding Common Ground for Multiparty Problems*. San Francisco: Jossey-Bass.
Straus, David. 2002. *How to Make Collaboration Work: Powerful Ways to Build Consensus, Solve Problems, and Make Decisions*. San Francisco: Berrett-Koehler Publishers.
Susskind, Lawrence, and Patrick Field. 1996. *Dealing with an Angry Public: The Mutual Gains Approach to Resolving Public Disputes*. San Francisco: Jossey-Bass.

Susskind, Lawrence, Sarah McKearnan, and Jennifer Thomas-Larmer. 1999. *Consensus Building Handbook.* Thousand Oaks, CA: Sage Publications.

Facilitation and Meeting Management
Moore, Christopher W. 2003. *The Mediation Process: Practical Strategies for Resolving Conflict,* 2nd ed. San Francisco: Jossey-Bass.
Schwarz, Roger. 2002. *The Skilled Facilitator.* San Francisco: Jossey-Bass.
Straus, David, and Michael Doyle. 1977. *How to Make Meetings Work.* New York: Jove/Berkeley/Penguin.

Negotiation and Dispute Resolution
Fisher, Roger, William Ury, and Bruce Patton. 1991. *Getting to YES: Negotiating Agreement Without Giving In,* 2nd ed. New York: Penguin.
Fisher, Roger, and Daniel Shapiro. 2005. *Beyond Reason:Using Emotions As You Negotiate.* New York: Viking.
Kolb, Deborah, and Judith Williams. 2000. *The Shadow Negotiation: How Women Can Master the Hidden Agendas That Determine Bargaining Success.* New York: Simon and Schuster.
Stone, Douglas, Bruce Patton, and Sheila Heen. 1999. *Difficult Conversations.* New York: Penguin.
Susskind, Lawrence, and Jeffrey Cruikshank. 1987. *Breaking the Impasse: Consensual Approaches to Resolving Public Disputes.* New York: Basic Books.
Ury, William. 1993. *Getting Past No: Negotiating your Way from Confrontation to Cooperation.* New York: Bantam Books.

Brainstorming and Value Creation
Adams, James. 1974. *Conceptual Blockbusting: A Guide to Better Ideas.* Cambridge, MA: Perseus Books.
DeBono, Edward. 1970. *Lateral Thinking: Creativity Step by Step.* New York: Harper and Row.
Lax, David A., and James K. Sebenius. 1986. *The Manager as Negotiator: Bargaining for Cooperation and Competitive Gain.* New York: Free Press.

CBA in the Private Sector
Cavenagh, Thomas. 1999. *Business Dispute Resolution: Best Practices in Systems Design and Case Management.* Winfield, KS: Southwestern College Press.
Walton, Richard, Joel Cutcher-Gershonfeld, and Robert McKersie. 1994. *Strategic Negotiations: A Theory of Change in Labor Relations.* Cambridge, MA: Harvard University Press.

Organizational Learning and Development
Argyris, Chris. 1992. *On Organizational Learning.* Malden, MA: Blackwell.
Senge, Peter. 1990. *The Fifth Discipline.* New York: Bantam, Doubleday, Dell.

Index